Taking it Easy

ANDY FENNER

Photography by
LAR LESLIE

SUNBIRD PUBLISHERS

When I first conceptualised this book I wanted to steer clear of clichés. So it sucks that I have to kick off with one. But I now understand why authors make dedications to family. I could never have done this without the support and encouragement of mine. I'd especially like to thank my gorgeous wife, Nicole. Her hugs and high fives kept me going whenever I began to doubt myself. She's a legend and I love her dearly.

CONTENTS

ANDY FENNER

Author, designer and freelance food writer

Taking It Easy is a gorgeous book that oozes style and substance, much like the author, whom I both admire and respect for his wholesome food philosophy. When I first met Andy he was a blogger – amongst many others – trying to make a name for himself and trying to find a career in food. His blog (written under the pseudonym Jamie Who) quickly became one of the most popular in the country and his rise from obscurity to well-respected food writer has been meteoric. Not satisfied with only writing about food, he now also consults in a branding and design capacity for a number of restaurants and wineries. Named as one of "200 Young South Africans to watch" by *Mail & Guardian* in 2010, Andy has emerged as one of the finest young talents in this country.

In this book he has chosen his 20 favourite chefs based on their own individual styles. He sums it up by explaining to me that "every chef has a strong food philosophy. Well … every good chef. The people in this book have that unique creative streak of genius that sets them apart. When you put them next to each other they become even cooler, as you can see their different approaches to food and the distinctive role it plays."

What makes this book especially refreshing for me is that it offers readers a rare and intimate glimpse into the kitchens and dining rooms of some of South Africa's best-loved chefs and foodies. A true culinary adventure, each chapter tells a different story, whether it's of following the award-winning David Higgs around Johannesburg's Neighbourgoods Market before watching him transform his spoils into a fabulously casual meal, or joining Margot Janse and her family at their Franschhoek home for a convivial table-side feast. Whatever the location, whomever the subject, the golden thread that runs through the pages of this book, is that good, honest food cooked with care and generosity can feed both body and soul. Narrated by Andy, whose special brand of wit comes alive on every page, he beautifully conveys what a humbling privilege it is to join his food heroes during their downtime, making us (the readers) feel honoured too.

Andy points out, quite rightly, that his photographer Lar Leslie deserves special credit. "I would never – and could never – have done this book without Lar. She is the next big thing in food photography for sure. She's a genius. Every single pic in this book was taken with natural lighting and no stylist. Most of them were done on the fly, with only one shot at getting it right. To have nailed every single shot the way she has is a miracle and it made my job very easy. She's special."

An absolutely stunning book, *Taking It Easy* is a true celebration of some of South Africa's biggest food stars. The author and photographer could well be rising stars too – hopefully this is the first of many from this dynamic duo who work so well together.

Abigail Donnelly, editor of 'Eat Out' and food editor of Woolworths 'Taste' magazine

Dear Jeff & Carol
Happy Coding
Julian Barns

BERTUS BASSON

Tomato risotto with buffalo mozzarella and waterblommetjies
Green bean and fennel salad
Beef stroganoff with gnocchi
Panna cotta with preserved fruit and caramel

When I first met Bertus Basson a few years back he had a wild Mohawk and swore like a sailor. Nowadays he's grown up a bit and his "hawk" has been replaced by a ponytail. I think it's a bit Eddie Vedder-ish, hinting still at the inner rock star chef.

Bertus operates from Overture (consistently ranked amongst South Africa's top restaurants by anyone who matters) and while his food might be simpler than in the past, it's better than ever. He's an ambitious dude and – if you manage to decipher the machine-gun explanations shooting out of his mouth – you'll hear that he has his hands full. Bertus and his business partner (fellow chef Craig Cormack) operate Sofia's on Morgenster as well as the quirky AmaZink Eatery in Khayamandi. They also have a catering company, conceptualising incredibly cool events and menus.

Bertus drops me a text a few days before I'm set to meet him for lunch. He says he's decided to host a Pinot Party, "Nothing fancy Andy, just six or seven of the country's best Pinot Noirs." Typical. Here's a guy who knows how to have a good time.

He's late for his own lunch, and comes strolling around the corner with his beloved dog, Patat. They've been to the park to walk off the dog's "ridiculous energy", as explained by Bertus. It's not lost on me that Bertus might also need a few trips round the park to slow down to normal speed. True to form, he has whipped everyone into his flat before I can even blink. And the wine is flowing. It's a great bunch of people and the common love of food eventually takes its toll. They want to be fed. Bertus eases into the kitchen and quickly throws together a risotto, not letting the fact that he has to cook get in the way of some good story-telling. I comment on the fact that he's not using stock, but water from a kettle instead. "This is government-issued stock, bru," is the reply. Classic. That's pretty much the theme for the rest of the lunch. Unpretentious, unfussy, honest cooking.

The risotto is finished off with some waterblommetjies, a few scoops of olive tapenade and torn chunks of mozzarella. A thick, glossy beef stroganoff is served with fluffy gnocchi. Delicate miniature panna cotta are lumped together in a big platter and dotted with pieces of preserved fruit that come from a variety of weird jars. "I get this stuff from my Auntie in Riebeek Kasteel. Honestly, it's the best I've had." The final flourish is a landslide of thick caramel sauce.

The party is in full swing now. Everyone is eating, laughing and celebrating … well … nothing in particular. Except each other's company. The Pinot Noir supply is dwindling. Bertus is eyeing a bottle of tequila. It's a good time to leave.

TOMATO RISOTTO

WITH BUFFALO MOZZARELLA AND WATERBLOMMETJIES | SERVES 4

THE SAUCE

- 1 onion, finely chopped
- 1 clove garlic, crushed
- olive oil
- 8 fresh tomatoes, puréed and passed through a sieve
- 300 g waterblommetjies

THE TOMATO RISOTTO

- 1 onion, finely chopped
- 2 cloves garlic, crushed
- a knob of butter
- 500 g Arborio rice
- 1 litre chicken stock
- 250 g buffalo mozzarella, torn into rough chunks
- 1 cup grated Parmesan cheese
- olive tapenade, for garnishing
- fresh basil leaves, for garnishing

Get a head start on the sauce by gently frying the onion and garlic in a little olive oil until softened, but not coloured. Add the tomato purée and reduce until it is the right consistency (you want it to coat the back of a spoon). Set aside.

Trim and clean the waterblommetjies, steam until tender and blanch. Set aside until the risotto is cooked and ready to assemble.

Now make the risotto. Gently fry the onion and garlic in a little butter until softened, but not coloured. Add your rice and cook until the rice kernels appear glassy.

Lower the heat and add one ladle of hot chicken stock, stirring well. The rice will absorb the stock. Then add another ladle and repeat the process for about 15 minutes, stirring gently so the rice doesn't stick to the bottom of the pot. Cook until the rice is still slightly firm to the bite, but not chalky.

When you're happy with the rice, stir in the tomato sauce, and add the waterblommetjies and the mozzarella. Stir in the Parmesan and an extra knob of butter, and mix until everything is creamy.

Spoon onto plates and serve garnished with scoops of tapenade and some fresh basil leaves.

TIP: Make sure that you wash your waterblommetjies properly. The intrusive crunch of pond grit would spoil all your hard work, so take a bit of time to trim the stalks and rinse the flowers well.

Dissolve a tablespoon of salt in a bowl of cold water and leave your waterblommetjies to soak in there for a few hours (preferably overnight). Drain and rinse the waterblommetjies several times until all traces of grit are gone.

GREEN BEAN AND FENNEL SALAD

SERVES 4

- 500 g fresh green beans
- 2 fennel bulbs
- 1 red onion
- olive oil
- balsamic vinegar
- salt and pepper
- lemon juice
- sugar (optional)

Bring a pot of salted water to the boil. Drop in the whole beans and cook for 2 minutes. Remove with a slotted spoon and plunge into a bowl of iced water. When cool, dry and split the beans. Set aside.

Slice the fennel and red onion as finely as possible (a mandolin slicer is ideal for this). Combine with the beans and transfer to a serving dish.

Make a vinaigrette by using a 3:1 ratio of olive oil to balsamic vinegar. Whisk to emulsify. Season well, add lemon juice to taste and a sprinkling of sugar if necessary.

Drizzle over the salad and use your hands to toss. This will ensure that everything is coated evenly.

BEEF STROGANOFF

WITH GNOCCHI | SERVES 4

THE BEEF STROGANOFF

- 750 g beef fillet, thinly sliced
- 2 cloves garlic, finely chopped
- 200 g mushrooms, sliced
- 2 green peppers, sliced
- 1 onion, sliced
- freshly picked thyme
- a knob of butter
- 250 ml beef stock
- a generous pinch of paprika
- 300 ml cream
- fresh parsley, to garnish

To make the stroganoff, heat a pan until very hot and sear the meat in batches. Set aside.

Sweat off the garlic, vegetables and thyme in butter on a medium heat for 15 minutes.

Add the stock, bring to the boil and reduce the heat. Cook until you're left with about half the amount of liquid.

Stir in the paprika, add the cream and bring to the boil. Reduce the heat and simmer gently until required.

THE GNOCCHI

- 500 g mashed potato
- 150 g flour
- 1 egg
- ½ teaspoon nutmeg
- ½ cup grated Parmesan
- a pinch of salt

To make the gnocchi, bring a pot of salted water to the boil. Mix together the mashed potato, flour, egg, nutmeg, Parmesan and salt. Work gently into a light dough.

Dust a clean work surface with some flour and roll out about 6 balls. Gently roll your dough into long, thin logs and cut them into pieces. (Half a thumb's length is a pretty good size.)

Cook the gnocchi in the boiling water, removing them with a slotted spoon as they rise to the surface.

To serve, add the gnocchi to the stroganoff and warm through. Spoon into bowls and garnish with finely chopped fresh parsley.

PANNA COTTA

WITH PRESERVED FRUIT AND CARAMEL | SERVES 4

THE PANNA COTTA

- 1 litre cream
- seeds from 2 vanilla pods
  (or 1 teaspoon vanilla paste)
- 180 g sugar
- 3 gelatine leaves, soaked in
  some cold water
- preserved fruit of your choice

Pour the cream into a pot and bring to the boil. Split the vanilla pods and scrape the seeds into the cream. Add the sugar and cook gently until dissolved. Remove from the heat.

Gently squeeze the gelatine leaves to drain excess water. Add to the hot cream mixture and stir until everything is combined. Pour the mixture into moulds of your choice and place in the fridge until set.

To serve, place a small plate upside-down on the moulds and flip over to allow the set mixture to slide out. Transfer individual servings carefully onto a large platter, dot with your favourite preserved fruit, and pour warm caramel sauce on top.

THE CARAMEL SAUCE

- 200 g sugar
- 200 ml cream
- 150 ml water
- 50 g butter, softened
- seeds from 2 vanilla pods

Pour the sugar into a pan and allow to melt gradually over medium heat. Do not stir, otherwise it will crystallise.

Once the caramel has formed, deglaze the pan with the cream and the water. Finally, stir in the butter and the vanilla.

Serve warm, poured liberally over the platter of panna cotta and fruit.

CHANTEL DARTNALL

Grilled duck red curry
Bags of gold
Sunburst pomelo salad
Hot and sour prawn soup

The Orient Hotel in Elandsfontein is like a modern-day oasis. The same colour as the red clay that it sits on, it is a colossal and imposing building. High arches, spiralled towers, oversized gates and opulent artefacts from the East make it even more surreal.

In this parallel world (where you could be anywhere from Cambodia to India) sits Mosaic, a restaurant run by the gorgeous Chantel Dartnall. The food she makes there is as special as the chef and the environment, as she draws inspiration from nature to create delicate, elegant food.

With her family home only a few minutes' walk from the hotel, the setting there is as you'd expect: more tributes to the East, with sculptures, carvings, paintings, carpets, pillows and a collection of Koi fish. It's astonishing stuff.

Chantel has had quite a morning, beginning with a panic-stricken text to me, explaining the power has gone out. Not ideal when you're planning a Thai feast. To pull off anything, let alone the ambitious menu she has planned, will be a massive achievement.

Not to worry. Chantel has improvised by taking blankets and a few cushions to create a spontaneous setting underneath a nearby tree. A tiny table is then packed with a variety of dishes, each bursting with colours. Chantel has just returned from Bangkok, where she managed to attend a few local cooking classes, and she speaks with passion about all she learnt. The consistency of the sauces, the addition of fruit to the curry, the flavour combinations and various techniques are all explained with obvious delight. She has added this to the many influences she has from Eastern cooking.

Chantel takes her guests through the meal. It is customary to bring everything to the table and have people eat whatever they want, however they see fit. No problem. The ladies climb into tom yum soup, a prawn, chicken and grapefruit salad, a duck red curry, and "money parcels" (crab and chicken wontons).

And then they do it all over again. They're easily able to climb in for seconds, with food this light. This fresh. This clean.

With the buffet coming to an end, the ladies seem to be lounging pretty deeply into those cushions. The blanket is scattered with empty plates and saucers. There is plenty of laughter and licking of fingers (a result of the sticky prawns). It's been a feast and she's pulled it off without electricity.

Told you she was special.

GRILLED DUCK RED CURRY

GAENG PHED PED YANG | SERVES 6

THE DUCK CURRY

- 6 duck breasts (*magret*)
- 8 cloves garlic, peeled
- 12 coriander roots and stems
- vegetable oil
- 8 tablespoons red curry paste
- 1 teaspoon ground coriander seeds
- pinch of ground cumin seeds
- 1 ½ litres coconut milk
- fish sauce, to taste
- 6 tablespoons sugar
- 6 kaffir lime leaves, finely sliced
- 30 grapes, deseeded
- 300 g pineapple, cut into small pieces
- 15 cherry tomatoes, halved
- 1 bunch Thai basil leaves
- 3 large red chillies, sliced

TO GARNISH

- 100 ml cream of coconut milk
- fresh basil leaves

Grill the duck under a very hot grill for about 4 minutes on each side, until it is half cooked. Slice and set aside.

Using a mortar and pestle, pound the garlic with the coriander roots and stems.

Heat the oil in a wok until very hot. Add the curry paste, pounded garlic and fresh coriander, the ground coriander seeds and the cumin. Stir fry for about 3 minutes.

Add the coconut milk a little at a time and bring to the boil. Add the fish sauce, sugar and kaffir lime leaves, simmer for 5 minutes, and then add the duck.

Add the grapes, pineapple pieces and cherry tomatoes, and simmer for a further minute. Stir in the Thai basil leaves and the red chilli.

Transfer to a serving pot, float the cream of coconut milk on top of the curry and sprinkle with some fresh basil leaves. Serve with fragrant steamed rice.

BAGS OF GOLD

THUNG THONG | MAKES 8 PIECES

THE FILLING

- 2 cloves garlic, peeled
- 2 coriander roots and stems
- 2 Chinese dried mushrooms
- 1 spring onion (scallion), finely sliced
- 160 g raw minced white chicken meat
- 30 g cooked crab meat
- 1 egg
- 1 ½ teaspoons Blue Elephant Special Sauce
- 1 teaspoon sugar
- ½ teaspoon ground white pepper
- pinch of salt

To make the filling, pound the garlic into a paste in a mortar with the coriander roots and stems. Soak the mushrooms for 10 minutes in cold water and slice finely.

Mix all the filling ingredients together in a bowl and knead well. Set aside.

THE BAGS

- 8 pieces dry bean curd pastry or spring roll pastry, each cut into 12 cm squares
- 8 spring onion (scallion) leaves, each about 15 – 18 cm long
- vegetable oil for deep frying

To make the bags, moisten the pastry in cold water. Place some of the filling in the centre of each piece and continue until you have divided the filling among the 8 pieces of pastry.

Soften the spring onion leaves by putting them briefly into hot water.

Form pouches by bringing the four corners of the pastry squares together above the filling and tying them together with the spring onion leaves. Deep-fry for 4 to 5 minutes in oil heated to 180 °C. Remove and drain on kitchen paper.

TO SERVE

- green salad leaves
- sweet chilli sauce, for dunking

Arrange the bags on a platter, toss some salad leaves in between and serve with sweet chilli sauce in a small bowl.

SUNBURST POMELO SALAD

YAM SAM-O | SERVES 6

THE SALAD

- 120 g desiccated coconut
- 12 pomelos (or 3 large ruby grapefruits)
- 1.2 kg cooked chicken breasts
- 1.2 kg cooked prawns
- 120 g ground dried shrimps
- 100 ml fresh lemon juice
- 3 tablespoons fish sauce
- 200 ml tamarind sauce
- 1 cup bean sprouts
- 12 – 15 lightly steamed asparagus spears
- 120 g roasted peanuts

THE GARNISH

- Thai basil leaves
- edible flowers (optional)

Sauté the desiccated coconut in a non-stick frying pan, without any oil, until light brown. Slice the grapefruits in two and, using the point of a sharp knife, carefully separate the segments and set them aside.

Remove the skin from the chicken breasts and cut them into cubes. Mix the cubed chicken, prawns and ground shrimps together in a bowl.

Mix the lemon juice, fish sauce and tamarind sauce together, and pour over the prawn mixture.

Add the toasted coconut, grapefruit segments, sprouts, asparagus (cut in half on the diagonal) and peanuts. Toss together lightly.

Transfer to a serving platter, and finish by scattering over the basil leaves and the flowers. Serve at room temperature.

CHEF'S NOTE: On my travels we used a beautifully sweet fruit called a pomelo. Locally, a grapefruit is just as good.

HOT AND SOUR PRAWN SOUP

TOM YUM | SERVES 6

TOM YUM

- 6 small green chillies
- 5 coriander roots and stems
- 1 litre chicken stock
- 15 thin slivers ginger
- 5 stems lemon grass, finely chopped
- 5 kaffir lime leaves
- 200 g small button mushrooms, quartered
- 18 king prawns, shelled, deveined and headless (tails attached)
- 4 tablespoons fish sauce
- 3 ½ tablespoons lemon juice

THE GARNISH

- fresh coriander leaves

In a mortar, crush the green chillies with the coriander roots and stems. Set aside.

Heat the stock to boiling point in a saucepan. Add the ginger, lemon grass, kaffir lime leaves and mushrooms, and bring back to the boil.

Add the prawns, fish sauce, crushed chillies and coriander roots and stems, and lemon juice. Simmer for 1 minute.

Serve hot in individual soup bowls, allowing 3 prawns per person. Sprinkle fresh coriander leaves over the broth just before serving.

CHRIS ERASMUS

Teriyaki pork belly
Caesar potato salad
Chris de Jager's peri-peri chicken
Michelle's chocolate Amarula mud cake

Having built up an enormous reputation at places like Ginja and Five Flies (when both were at their peak), Chris Erasmus is known in South Africa for his nose-to-tail approach to eating.

It might well have something to do with growing up in the Karoo, where his childhood lessons were slightly different from most. Whereas most kids would prefer a Nintendo Wii as an afternoon treat, things like how to butcher a lamb, how to preserve fruit and how to cook tripe were standard distractions for Chris. It's no wonder that he puts such a strong emphasis on the provenance of his food and, in his new position as head chef at the acclaimed Pierneef à la Motte, he drives this message home every day.

Chris has asked us to come to his place at 4 pm on a Sunday. If you're thinking that's a bit late, well … so was I.

"Dude, I've got to do a lunchtime shift," is his exasperated explanation. "We work out here in Franschhoek!"

After a pretty tricky drive from Cape Town (where we dealt with some torrential rain and lightning) we pull in outside his house. It's usually at this point that I try to guess what the chef will be cooking and today my money is on a hearty stew. Imagine my surprise when I get out the car and am greeted with the unmistakable smell of burning wood. Surely not? Yup.

Chris is hovering underneath his protected porch with three separate braais of various sizes and forms blazing. Glass of bubbly in one hand, tongs in the other, I issue my nod of respect.

The day is hilarious. At one stage about 25 people are there, and each has brought (on average) four or five bottles of wine. The team seems intent on finishing it all. What's interesting is how many other local chefs are guests. Chris explains the camaraderie that exists within the community. "We all try and get together as often as possible to swap war stories," he explains.

It's awesome to see. Kids are jumping in puddles and dogs seem to be on every spare seat. Chris's wife Alisha takes it all in her stride, herself having worked in the restaurant industry for many years.

Teriyaki pork belly is first to hit the grid. It's a flurry of activity from there, as each chef has a turn poking and prodding anything that comes near the fire. Which includes some peri-peri spatchcock chickens, basted with a secret recipe. Fresh bread from the restaurant and some preserved fruit from Chris's mom in the Karoo also get hoovered up. A chocolate torte doesn't stand a chance.

We slip away, promising to return. Next time I'm booking a B&B. I hate missing a party like the one that's about to kick off.

If this is how much fun they have under those conditions, I'd love to see them when the sun comes out.

TERIYAKI PORK BELLY

SERVES 8

- 1.5 kg free-range pork belly, skin on
- 1 litre chicken stock
- 2 tablespoons chopped ginger
- 4 cloves garlic
- 1 stick lemon grass
- 1 cup chopped coriander
- 500 ml dark soy sauce
- 500 ml mirin
- 250 ml sake
- 1 tablespoon fermented black bean sauce
- 2 teaspoons cornflour

You need to plan ahead a little for this recipe as the pork belly should soak in the marinade for 2 days before you cook it.

Score the skin of the belly by making incisions across the length of the meat, about 5 mm apart.

Place the chicken stock, ginger, garlic, lemon grass and coriander in a saucepan and reduce by half over high heat. Pour the sauce through a strainer and return the liquid to the saucepan.

Add the soy sauce, mirin, sake and black bean sauce, and bring back to the boil. Mix the cornflour with 2 tablespoons of water and pour into the boiling liquid. Simmer for 2 minutes then remove from the heat.

Allow to cool completely. Place the belly in a plastic packet or airtight container and pour in the marinade. Leave in the refrigerator for 2 days.

To cook in a Weber, place the belly skin-side down over medium coals and close the lid. Only after 30 minutes, lift the lid and turn the belly. Cook for another hour with the lid on and remove the belly from the heat. Allow to rest for 10 minutes then carve.

NOTE: Fermented black bean sauce is readily available from most supermarkets.

CAESAR POTATO SALAD

SERVES 6

THE DRESSING

- 2 egg yolks
- 1 teaspoon lemon juice
- salt and pepper, to taste
- 1 teaspoon mustard
- 1 teaspoon preserved lemon
- 1 teaspoon cream
- 2 anchovy fillets, very finely chopped
- 300 ml oil (grape seed or mild olive blend)
- 60 ml water

Place the egg yolks, lemon juice, salt, pepper, mustard, preserved lemon, cream and anchovies in a bowl. Whisk and add the oil, only a few drops at a time, until everything is emulsified.

Taste and adjust the seasoning if necessary. Add the water, also only a little bit at a time, until the desired consistency is reached. Set aside.

THE SALAD

- 1 kg baby potatoes, washed
- 1 tablespoon vegetable oil
- 1 tablespoon butter
- ½ cup bacon, diced
- ½ cup brown mushrooms, diced
- 2 mielies, cooked and kernels stripped from the cob
- 200 g fine beans, blanched and roughly chopped
- ½ red onion, finely chopped
- 1 tablespoon chives, finely chopped
- salt and pepper, to taste
- ½ teaspoon black truffle oil

Place the potatoes in a pot and top with cold water. Add salt and bring to the boil, simmering until cooked. Drain the potatoes and leave to cool. Carefully peel the skins with a sharp knife and quarter each potato.

Heat a pan and add the oil and the butter. Add the bacon and mushrooms, and cook until golden brown. Remove from the pan and discard the oil.

Mix all the vegetables, the bacon and the chives until well combined, and add enough dressing to coat the salad evenly. Season with salt and pepper, and drizzle over the truffle oil.

CHRIS DE JAGER'S PERI-PERI CHICKEN

SERVES 4 – 6

- 200 ml white wine
- 100 ml sunflower oil
- 100 ml lemon juice, freshly squeezed
- 6 teaspoons high-quality paprika
- 2 teaspoons peri-peri powder
- 1 red chilli, finely chopped
- 1 free-range chicken, spatchcocked

Mix all the ingredients together and rub onto the chicken. Refrigerate for 24 hours.

Braai over medium coals, turning frequently and basting the chicken with the marinade. Season with salt, if necessary.

MICHELLE'S CHOCOLATE AMARULA

MUD CAKE | SERVES 8 – 10

- 180 g treacle sugar
- 180 g caramel sugar
- 6 eggs
- 250 ml fresh cream
- 360 g dark chocolate (the very best you can get, 70 % cocoa)
- 360 g unsalted butter
- 60 ml Amarula liqueur
- 200 g digestive biscuits
- 100 g unsalted butter, melted
- 1 tablespoon cocoa powder

Preheat the oven to 160 °C. Place the sugar and eggs in a large bowl and beat until light and airy. Add the cream to the egg mixture and incorporate slowly.

Place the chocolate and 360 g butter in a heat-proof bowl and place over a pot of water on a gentle boil. Once the chocolate and butter have melted, add to the egg mixture. Stir the Amarula into the mix.

Place the digestive biscuits in a food processor and pulse to form a powder. (If you don't have a processor, place them in a tea towel and crush with a rolling pin.) Pour your melted butter onto your biscuit powder, mix and use to form a base in a 20 cm springform cake tin. Press the base tightly down in an even layer and place in the oven for 5 minutes. Remove and press down again.

Pour the chocolate mixture onto the base and bake for 40 minutes – it will look raw but take it out! Leave to set in the refrigerator overnight and serve at room temperature with your favourite ice cream.

DAVID HIGGS

Fresh tuna with oysters, sea salt, micro radish and lime
Salad of shaved fennel with chorizo and oven-roasted olives
Goat's cheese with dark chocolate and balsamic syrup

When David Higgs (former *Eat Out* chef of the year) announced that he would be leaving Rust en Vrede (former *Eat Out* restaurant of the year), the country's culinary community waited in anticipation to see where he'd be heading. When he announced he was leaving Cape Town to spearhead the food team at Radisson Blu Gautrain Hotel in Joburg, it was quite a shock. David was trading in an intimate, fine-dining restaurant in the winelands for a contemporary, slick, modern hotel restaurant. Under the name Central One Bar & Restaurant, he'd be serving at least 300 covers a day, and he'd be overseeing every bit of food that came out of the kitchen. It was a massive task.

At the time of writing, David was already on his way to transforming the hotel and putting it squarely on the map as one of the city's best eating options. More importantly, he was falling in love with Joburg. So much so that when I asked him how he wanted to do this shoot he explained that in his free time he likes to get out and explore his new home, instead of "sitting around". That attitude is typical of the guy – he never stops looking for inspiration and ideas.

And we find both of those things at the newly opened Neighbourgoods Market in Juta Street. Sipping a beer and taking in the skyline, he says I should order another one while he heads off to get some ingredients. We've decided to do

a little bit of urban foraging, and create a meal with whatever catches David's eye.

By the time I get back with beer number two, the first dish is basically done. Beautiful tuna, thinly sliced and dressed with fresh lime juice, sits between naked oysters and baby radishes. Light, fresh and perfectly balanced; a brilliant dish.

A salad is knocked up next. Again using ingredients that he's picked up since arriving, it takes less than 10 minutes from start to finish. Salty olives marry with sliced chorizo, while fresh shaved fennel and cherry tomatoes bring sweetness. Cheese is shaved and combined with pine nuts to add texture. It looks incredible on a plate but really it's just a combination of great produce. "Inspiration is easy when you're having fun," smiles David as he steps back to admire his work.

His ability to combine flavours is highlighted in the dessert. Chunky torn bread, chalky goat's cheese and dark chocolate are arranged on a board and drizzled with pistachios and aged balsamic vinegar. Not an obvious dish, but an unforgettable one.

The shoot is getting plenty of attention and David takes it in his stride, offering free samples and at one stage bartering some of the tuna and oysters for more beer (sheer genius). The guy is pretty special and his passion for good produce has been a privilege to watch. There's no doubt about it … Cape Town's loss is Joburg's gain.

FRESH TUNA WITH OYSTERS

SEA SALT, MICRO RADISH AND LIME | SERVES 4

– 300 g yellowfin or longfin tuna
  (pole-caught only)
– coarse sea salt
– 12 medium oysters (West coast
  oysters are best)
– 80 g micro radishes (if you can't get
  these, slice normal radish)
– 2 tablespoons olive oil
– 6 limes, quartered

Slice the tuna into thin pieces and sprinkle liberally with salt.
Shuck the oysters (or have your fishmonger do this for you)
and arrange with the tuna on a platter.

Coat your radish in some olive oil and scatter onto the
platter. Drizzle with the rest of the oil, and finish by squeezing
over the lime juice.

There are some really good local cured meats available nowadays. Don't be shy to question the provenance by asking the producer where the animals are raised.

SALAD OF SHAVED FENNEL

WITH CHORIZO AND OVEN-ROASTED OLIVES | SERVES 2

THE ROASTED OLIVES

- 500 g black olives, pips in and pierced with a fork
- 80 ml olive oil
- 20 g fresh rosemary, roughly chopped
- 2 cloves garlic, roughly chopped

Preheat your oven to 160 °C. Toss all the ingredients together and tip into a roasting tray. Bake until wilted. Cool, bottle and use as required.

These delicious olives will lift any salad to new heights and are just as good stirred through wet polenta or crispy, roasted potatoes.

THE DRESSING

- 250 ml extra virgin olive oil
- juice and zest of 3 lemons

Whisk until well combined. Drizzle over the salad just before serving.

THE FENNEL SALAD

- 1 medium-sized fennel bulb, thinly sliced or shaved on a mandolin slicer
- 100 g cherry tomatoes, halved
- 60 g chorizo, thinly sliced
- 60 g roasted olives
- 4 tablespoons dressing
- 40 g strong, firm cheese, ideally cut on a girolle shaver (or just thinly sliced)
- 15 g pine nuts
- salt flakes
- freshly cracked black pepper

Arrange the fennel shavings and cherry tomatoes on a serving platter. Scatter the chorizo and roasted olives over the top, and drizzle with the dressing.

As a final touch, add your cheese and pine nuts. Season well and serve immediately.

GOAT'S CHEESE

WITH DARK CHOCOLATE AND BALSAMIC SYRUP | SERVES 4

THE BALSAMIC SYRUP

- 250 ml high-quality balsamic vinegar
- 2 tablespoons honey

Combine in a small saucepan and reduce over medium heat until it coats the back of a spoon lightly. Be careful not to make it too sticky, remembering that it will thicken as it cools. When cool, decant into a bottle, chill and use as required.

THE GOAT'S CHEESE

- 100 g best-quality dark chocolate
- 250 g semi-hard or hard goat's cheese, broken into chunks
- 30 g ripped and slightly toasted ciabatta
- 20 g salted pistachio nuts
- 1 tablespoon reduced balsamic syrup

Melt the chocolate in a bowl over gently simmering hot water and cool to room temperature. Arrange the cheese and ciabatta toast on a wooden board, and scoop the cooled chocolate on top. Scatter with the pistachio nuts, drizzle with the balsamic syrup and tuck in.

TIP: David used Honest Raw Chocolate, which he scooped from a jar – great if you can find it, but if you can't, melted best-quality dark chocolate will work just as well. But don't cut corners with the quality of the chocolate. You need something expensive and pure, with a high fat and cocoa count. Cheap chocolate is full of sugar and won't have the same effect.

FRANCK DANGEREUX

Saldanha Bay oysters with a ginger salsa
Tuna tartare with pine nuts and basil
Grilled kabeljou with fennel fondue
Sirloin flat bread sandwiches
Stone fruits and berries amandine

It's the classic story. French guy studies to be a chef. Guy works beneath some of the best teachers in the world. Guy opens a restaurant. Restaurant becomes best in Africa. Guy buys a barn and opens a bistro. Guy starts … whoaaah, hang on. He bought a barn?

Yes. He bought a barn. The guy in the story is Franck Dangereux and the restaurant was/is La Colombe, which he took to number 28 in the world according to the annual San Pellegrino World's 50 Best Restaurants list. So a family-friendly, chilled bistro in Noordhoek wasn't what most people expected next. But that's exactly what he did. And The Foodbarn was born.

Having met now business partner Pete de Bruin at a bar, the idea for an unpretentious restaurant that served elegant and tasty food was dreamt up over a bottle of tequila. It just might be the best thing ever to come from a bottle of tequila, because today The Foodbarn is brilliant. Capturing exactly what the two men originally discussed, food is clean and simple, with sauces and French techniques taking centre stage. There's a passion in the kitchen, with food that could be at any one of the more "illustrious" venues around the country. It's brilliant in its simplicity.

Franck's home is just as chilled as his restaurant. With a distinctly French Provençal feel, sky-blue shutters hang off a stone house, conveniently facing the sea and sporting a view that makes it pretty difficult to be uptight about anything.

Franck's wife, Sammy, plays the perfect hostess too, welcoming guests while managing to keep everyone's glasses full. She takes us for a quick spin around the garden, which itself is pretty interesting when you consider the pets: dogs, horses, a pig, cats and a handful of chickens.

Lunch is like some kind of culinary pantomime, with wild gestures, a couple of "I told you so" looks, and warm, contented smiles washing over everybody's faces.

As the wine goes down, guests begin what I will later learn is a fairly common game of basically just taking the piss out of Franck's accent. There's a lot of laughter at this point. Like … a lot of it. A particularly good story about Franck's struggle to differentiate between the words "booze" and "boobs" brings the house down.

And while all of this goes down, food somehow keeps turning up. Oysters are freshly shucked and dressed with a ginger and coriander salsa. Some of the guests have their first stab at the creature, but those same guests end up having three or four. I have about twelve. It's hard work writing a book. Fresh cob is pan-fried, beautiful sirloin is cooked on the braai and sliced onto toasted flat breads, tuna tartare is simply dressed and plated. Nectarines are stoned, drowned in custard and baked.

It's honest food, it's delicious food. It's the type of food – I'm sure – that Franck and Pete had in mind when they were enjoying that bottle of tequila.

49

FRESH SALDANHA BAY OYSTERS

WITH A GINGER AND CORIANDER SALSA | MAKES 24

- 24 oysters, shucked
- 1 tablespoon grated ginger
- 3 tablespoons chopped coriander
- 1 red chilli, finely sliced
- ½ teaspoon fish sauce
- 2 tablespoons fresh lime juice
- 5 tablespoons sunflower oil
- extra lime wedges, to serve

Make sure that the oysters are carefully cleaned.

Combine the remaining ingredients, apart from the extra lime wedges, and blitz in a food processor. (If you don't have one, just use a pestle and mortar).

Arrange the oysters on a large platter, throw on the extra lime wedges and spoon the salsa into a bowl to serve alongside them. Let your guests help themselves and encourage them to slurp straight from the shells.

TUNA TARTARE

WITH PINE NUTS AND BASIL | SERVES 4

- 8 tablespoons chopped basil
- 8 tablespoons good olive oil
- salt and black pepper, to taste
- 400 g fresh yellowfin tuna loin, bright red with the fat removed
- 4 tablespoons pine nuts, toasted
- zest and juice of 1 lime
- salt, to taste
- extra olive oil, to taste
- 4 handfuls watercress, washed
- soy sauce

Place the basil and olive oil in a blender, season with salt and pepper and blitz. Set aside.

Meanwhile, cut the tuna into ½ cm cubes and place in a salad bowl, along with the pine nuts, the zest and juice of the lime, some salt to taste and a generous swig of olive oil. Mix everything thoroughly so that each piece of fish is coated with oil.

To serve, spoon the tartare onto individual plates, top with watercress, drizzle with the basil salsa, and finish with a few drops of soy sauce per portion.

GRILLED KABELJOU

WITH FENNEL FONDUE, VINE TOMATOES AND TARRAGON CREAM | SERVES 4

THE FENNEL FONDUE
- 2 large bulbs fennel, washed and thinly sliced
- 1 tablespoon butter
- olive oil
- salt and pepper, to taste

In a large frying pan, fry the sliced fennel in the butter and a splash of oil for a few minutes, over a gentle heat. Add enough water to cover the fennel and cook slowly until evaporated. The fennel will be beautifully soft.

Finish by seasoning with salt and pepper. Set aside and keep warm until needed.

THE TARRAGON CREAM
- 300 ml cream
- 2 tablespoons white wine vinegar
- 2 tablespoons chopped fresh tarragon
- 40 g butter
- salt, to taste

Place the cream and vinegar in a saucepan, bring to the boil and reduce until the consistency thickens. Add the tarragon and the butter, season with salt and blitz with a hand blender. Keep warm.

THE KABELJOU
- 4 bunches of baby tomatoes, on the vine
- salt
- pepper
- olive oil
- 4 x 150 g pieces of fresh kabeljou, skin on
- 2 handfuls podded broad beans, blanched

Place the tomatoes on an oven tray, season and drizzle with enough oil to coat every tomato, once shaken. Place under a preheated grill in the oven for a few minutes, until their skins pop. Remove and keep warm.

Meanwhile, season the fish on both sides and rub with a little oil. In a hot, non-stick pan, fry the fish skin-side first until golden brown. Turn the fish and cook further. The time depends on the thickness of the fish but don't be tempted to overcook it. It shouldn't take more than a few minutes.

Allow the fish to rest for a minute or two before serving. To assemble, spoon some fennel fondue into the middle of the plate and carefully place your fish on top. Place your vine tomatoes on the side, scatter some of the beautiful broad beans onto the plate and finish with some of the tarragon sauce spooned over.

SIRLOIN FLAT BREAD SANDWICHES

WITH FRESH GARDEN HERBS | MAKES AT LEAST 10 SANDWICHES

THE FLAT BREAD
- 500 g Eureka Mills bread flour
- ½ sachet instant dry yeast
- ½ tablespoon salt
- 1 tablespoon sugar
- 300 ml water

Combine all the bread ingredients and mix well, before allowing to rest for 10 minutes. Turn out the dough onto a floured surface and cut into smallish pieces, to be rolled and shaped into balls. Place on a tray and allow to prove until doubled in size (about 40 minutes).

When risen, flatten to about ½ cm thick on a floured work surface, using a rolling pin. Bake directly on the grid over the braai until cooked through.

THE SIRLOIN
- 800 g free-range sirloin, trimmed, with thin layer of fat still on
- salt and pepper, to taste
- 2 tablespoons chilli flakes
- olive oil
- 4 handfuls mixed seasonal herbs
- balsamic vinegar, to taste
- freshly chopped chilli, as required

Season the beef with salt, pepper and chilli flakes, and rub with olive oil. Cook on the braai, turning quite often so that it doesn't burn. Cook to your liking and allow to rest for 10 minutes.

Coarsely chop all your herbs on a very large cutting board, adding lots of olive oil and balsamic vinegar, as well as salt and pepper, directly onto the board (you can use a tray if you don't have a big enough board). Franck used all the herbs in his garden for these sandwiches – try any combination of parsley, chives, basil, marjoram, dill, chervil, mint, coriander, tarragon or rocket.

Slice the meat and place it, with its juices, on top of the herbs. Add the fresh chilli and mix well. Serve by stuffing the flat breads with the meat and herb mixture.

TIP: Just do your thing by filling those little breads with meat and stacks of herbs and juices. Eat with your hands and make sure you mess on your chin …

STONE FRUITS AND BERRIES

AMANDINE | **SERVES 4**

THE AMANDINE

- 2 egg yolks
- 40 g castor sugar
- 25 g extremely finely ground almonds
- 100 ml whipped cream

Cream the yolks and sugar together until smooth. Add the ground almonds and mix well before folding in the whipped cream. Keep aside.

THE FRUIT

- 1 ripe nectarine
- 1 ripe peach
- 2 ripe apricots
- 1 punnet strawberries
- 1 punnet raspberries
- 2 tablespoons treacle sugar
- a little freshly chopped lemon verbena

Cut the stone fruit into quarters, removing the pips, and arrange them cut-side up on a heat-proof serving dish. Scatter over the berries. Sprinkle with the treacle sugar and some chopped lemon verbena (mint would also be good).

Now pour over the amandine mix and cook au gratin under the grill, making sure the dish isn't too near the element. Grill until golden brown – this will only take a few minutes.

Remove and serve with dollops of ice cream. I love lemon verbena ice cream, but you can use a good-quality vanilla.

GIORGIO NAVA

Beef carpaccio / Risotto Milanese
La Fiorentina / Tiramisu

Chefs are pushed for time. All the time. But none more so than Giorgio Nava. The guy is an Italian wrecking ball, smashing his way through the food scene in Cape Town with seemingly no intention of slowing down.

95 Keerom Street came first. Serving real Italian food, with authentic Milanese traditions, Giorgio wasn't catering for the guy who wanted a bowl of pasta with a thick red sauce. There weren't any chequered tablecloths. Instead, clean food was served in a masculine, minimalist environment. Flavours were concentrated and pronounced. The food was refreshingly simple. Ingredients were the stars. Carne came next, as a shrine to meat. Not long after that, Down South popped up in Long Street, dishing out prawns and ribs to the late-night party crowd.

On the other end of the sliding scale, Caffe Milano opened its doors, serving airy pastries and breads. Then? Mozzarella Bar. Serving … yip, mozzarella. Silky, smooth, soft mozzarella. If anybody needed convincing of how simple good Italian food can be, this hole-in-the-wall was it.

So, fitting in a shoot with Giorgio was always going to be a push. And when we arrive at his house in Camps Bay and ring the bell to no response, there's definitely a bit of panic. No need though. Two minutes later Giorgio's car pulls in behind us and out hop three beautiful dogs. "Myee babeeees," he gushes. "Iva jus takeen them for da walk een da mountains." The gesture as he says this, sweeping across the mountain in the background, is typically Italian. He's impossibly cool, this dude.

We head inside. His house is all about clean lines and neutral colours. "So, Giorgio, where are the guests?" I ask. And that's when everything goes quiet. Giorgio explains over the next few minutes that he thought the plan was to cook *as if* guests were coming. Not to actually invite them! I'm sensing a crisis, and hesitantly ask whether we should reschedule. "Absolutely not," is the emphatic reply, as places are set for Lar and me. It seems we are going to be his guests for the day and – without skipping a beat – he gets to work.

Not in the kitchen, mind you, but on the braai. Soon a fire is blazing and he's prepping the biggest, baddest, most beautiful chunk of meat I've seen. Calling this a T-Bone is like calling a Ferrari a Fiat.

As with his philosophy in all his restaurants, he keeps things laughably simple when he prepares the meat. "Olive oil. Salt. Pepper. Rosemary." The point is underlined with another one of those Italian gestures, this one indicating that anyone who does anything more to a piece of meat is a fool. When cooked, he carves it off the bone and sets it on a platter.

Then it's a risotto, cooked (astonishingly) in a pressure cooker. Noticing my shock, Giorgio asks me to trust him. The dish speaks for itself and is as good as any risotto I've eaten. Ever. I'm getting ready to leave the table when Giorgio slips a plate of tiramisu in front of me. Clearly he had it hiding in the fridge.

As I eat, he talks about his favourite food memories. Everything sounds better in Italian. I genuinely wonder where he gets the energy. With Giorgio, it's never a case of whether or not there'll be another project. It's only a matter of what it will be.

61

BEEF CARPACCIO

SERVES 4

– 100 ml extra virgin olive oil
– 1 whole egg
– 1 teaspoon lemon juice
– 1 teaspoon Worcestershire sauce
– salt and pepper, to taste
– 300 g chilled beef sirloin
– rocket leaves, to garnish
– Parmesan shavings, to garnish

Mix everything, except the meat, in a bowl until well combined.

Slice the meat as thinly as possible, and arrange on a plate, so that the slices overlap.

Spoon over the dressing and garnish with rocket leaves, Parmesan shavings and some extra olive oil.

RISOTTO MILANESE

SAFFRON RISOTTO | **SERVES 4 – 6**

– 1.2 litres chicken stock
– 400 g Arborio rice
– 1 heaped teaspoon saffron strands
– 100 g butter
– 150 g grated Parmesan cheese

In the pressure cooker, add the hot stock, the rice and the saffron. Close the pot and place the cooker on the stove over a very low heat. When it begins to whistle, time 7 minutes. When the time is up, release the valve, open the lid and add the butter along with the Parmesan cheese. Stir gently and serve.

LA FIORENTINA
24 MONTHS GRASS-FED BEEF T-BONE | SERVES 2

- 1.2 kg T-bone
- ½ cup extra virgin olive oil
- 20 g sea salt
- 10 g freshly cracked black pepper
- 4 cloves garlic, sliced
- 50 g rosemary

Massage the meat with the oil, salt, pepper, garlic and rosemary. Make sure that both sides are nicely coated.

Prepare a hot grill and cook for 20 minutes (for medium rare), turning every 5 minutes. Alternatively, cook over hot coals for 20 minutes, turning every 5 minutes. Allow the meat to rest for a few minutes, and then slice off the bone. Carve into slices and arrange on a platter, around the bone.

TIRAMISU

SERVES 4

- 1 box boudoir biscuits
- 1 cup filter coffee
- 1 tub mascarpone cheese
- 3 eggs, separated
- 2 tablespoons castor sugar
- cocoa powder, for dusting

Dip the biscuits quickly in the coffee (don't let them get soggy) and place in the dish, making sure they are packed together tightly. Place the mascarpone, egg yolks and sugar into a mixing bowl and whisk until smooth.

Beat the egg whites until they form stiff peaks. Fold the egg whites into the mascarpone mixture and pour over the soaked biscuits. Place in the fridge and allow to set.

To serve, dust with cocoa powder.

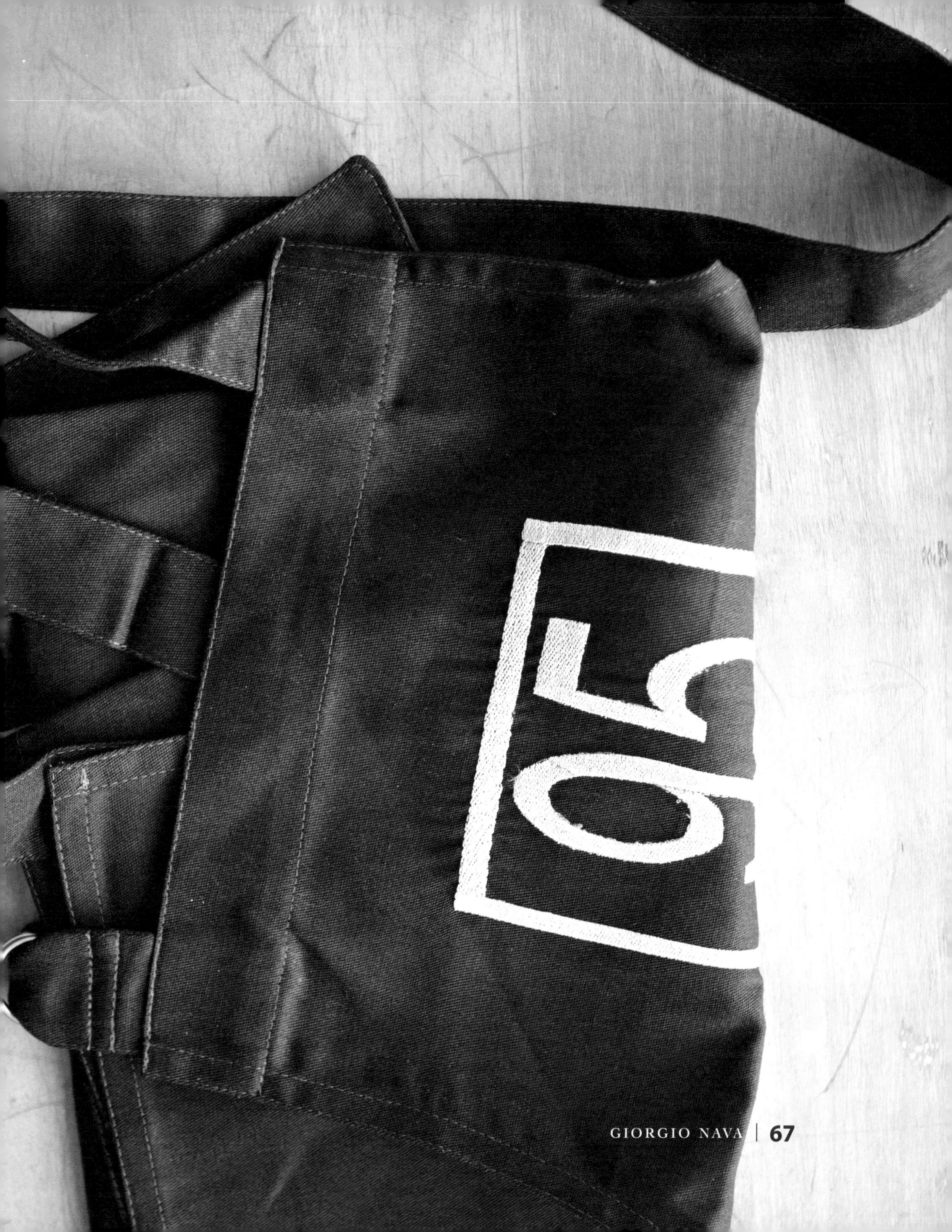

JASON LILLEY

Fresh green salad with gooseberry vinaigrette
Oven-roasted wing rib
Truffled baby potatoes & Sautéed asparagus
Ruby grapefruit crème brûlée

There aren't too many people who can take a storeroom, cut a hole in a wall and somehow turn it into a restaurant. But that's pretty much what Jason Lilley did. At the time (working underneath George Jardine's celebrated restaurant) he and his team of bakers got up at 4 am and religiously pumped out pies, croissants, sourdough, ciabatta and muffins. Every. Day. Of. The. Working. Week. 4 am people. It takes a special kind of commitment to do that.

Things have changed slightly since then. 2011 saw Jason making a big move. When Jardine closed its doors, Jason saw an opportunity to expand his "hatch". He took over the entire floor and opened his own show. Simply titled Jason Bakery, he opened to queues in the street. A simple space, with exposed wooden beams as cladding, it now feels like the sort of place you'd find in London, New York or Paris. Or in a Scandinavian sauna. The same legendary croissants are flying out, but so are more advanced dishes. The energy in his store is electric.

If you ever need to show an overseas visitor a real Cape Town CBD eating experience, this would be a good place to start. Jason might be built like some of the ovens he cooks with, but his touch is delicate and his palate is sharp (even if his consistently bad puns are not). Don't let the tattoos fool you – this guy is a serious cook.

On the day of our lunch, summer is letting her hair down for the first time. Now, for those of you who don't know, after a wet winter Capetonians lose their minds a bit at the first glimpse of sun. Deadlines cease to exist. Work hours are optional. The beach is flooded with people. Bars spill into streets. And Sunday afternoons (like the one we are enjoying) become Friday nights.

Jason is a natural host and, even with the sun spilling into a beautiful living room with stunning views, everyone finds themselves crammed into a tiny kitchen. Not a problem. That's where the beer is.

Jason's got some of his baking mates (Trav and Andrew) with him to help prep some of the other dishes and pretty soon the fresh salad is done, a tangy gooseberry vinaigrette is in the fridge and an enormous, dinosaurish hunk of wing rib is in the oven. He has somehow managed to prep all of this in minutes.

Eventually we do manage to assemble at the table with the views. It's hard to appreciate them with the distractions on the plates though. Potato salad is dressed with generous splashes of truffle extract, meat is carved, salads are dished, wine is poured. By the time the ruby grapefruit crème brûlées are being cracked, it's proved to be an epic lunch.

Jason leans back, folds those enormous arms and suggests we go somewhere for a drink. I consider mentioning the fact that the following day is Monday. It's too late for that … he's halfway out the door.

FRESH GREEN SALAD

WITH GOOSEBERRY VINAIGRETTE | SERVES 8

THE DRESSING

- 250 ml white wine vinegar
- ½ cup dried gooseberries
- 1 clove garlic, peeled
- 750 ml extra virgin olive oil
- salt, to taste
- freshly cracked black pepper, to taste

Make the dressing first. Heat the vinegar until it is about to start boiling. Add the gooseberries and allow them to steep for 10 minutes.

Pour into a blender, add the garlic and blitz until smooth. Add the olive oil slowly, incorporating it into the dressing. Season to taste and decant.

Set aside until needed.

THE SALAD

- 250 g rocket
- 250 g baby spinach
- ½ cup dried gooseberries
- 70 g toasted and roughly chopped cashews
- salt, to taste
- freshly cracked black pepper, to taste
- 100 g shaved Parmesan

Place the greens in a large bowl and scatter the gooseberries over the top. Add the dressing, using your hands to toss the salad to ensure that everything is well coated.

Transfer to a large platter, sprinkle with the toasted cashews and season to taste. Scatter over the Parmesan. Serve with extra bread to mop up the dressing.

OVEN-ROASTED WING RIB

SERVES 8 – 10

- 1 large wing rib, on the bone
- 3 sprigs thyme
- 3 sprigs rosemary
- 6 cloves garlic, peeled
- olive oil
- Maldon salt
- freshly ground black pepper

Score the meat about 1 cm deep along the top side, starting between each of the bones. Place a sprig of thyme, rosemary and 2 very lightly crushed garlic cloves in each of the scores. Rub the surface of the meat with olive oil and season well.

In a hot pan, seal off the meat. Transfer to a roasting pan and place in an oven at 170 °C for 2 hours. (You want the meat to be no less than medium-rare due to the fat content.)

When done, remove the meat from the roasting pan and allow it to rest for a while. Meanwhile, add a splash of wine to the cooking juices in the pan and reduce to create a beautiful sauce. After a few minutes, when the sauce has thickened, remove from the heat and keep warm.

To serve, slice the meat from the bone and spoon onto plates. As a final flourish, drizzle over some of the meat juices that you've turned into the incredible sauce. Serve with truffled baby potatoes and sautéed asparagus (see recipes on page 75).

TRUFFLED BABY POTATOES

SERVES 8 – 10

- 2 kg baby potatoes
- 300 g unsalted butter, softened
- 50 g flat leaf parsley, finely chopped
- 250 g Parmesan, grated
- ½ teaspoon truffle aroma oil
- Maldon salt
- freshly ground white pepper

Boil the potatoes until cooked. Drain and place back in the pot. Briefly place the pot back on the stove over a low heat, to cook off any remaining water. Remove from the stove.

Crush the baby potatoes and add the remaining ingredients. Gently mix until combined and serve with the wing rib (see recipe on page 73).

SAUTÉED ASPARAGUS

SERVES 8 – 10

- 3 punnets asparagus
- 50 g unsalted butter
- juice of 1 lemon
- Maldon salt
- freshly ground black pepper

Cut the dry, hard ends off the asparagus and peel from the base of the tips to the end of the stalk. Melt the butter in a frying pan and sauté the asparagus until cooked, but still with a slight bite.

Add the lemon juice and seasoning. Toss very gently and serve alongside the wing rib (see recipe on page 73).

RUBY GRAPEFRUIT CRÈME BRÛLÉE

SERVES 10

- 1 ruby grapefruit
- 2 vanilla pods, split in half, seeds scraped out
- 1.3 litres cream
- 7 whole eggs
- 200 g castor sugar
- muscovado sugar, for sprinkling

Using a vegetable peeler, peel the rind off the grapefruit. Add the rind, along with the vanilla pods, the seeds and the cream to a large pot. Gently heat the cream on the stove, being careful that it doesn't boil.

Combine the eggs and the sugar until just mixed. When the cream is at 80 °C, remove from the heat. Remove the grapefruit rind and vanilla pods, and pour a quarter of the cream into the egg mixture, combining well. Pour the egg mixture back into the rest of the cream and return to a low heat.

Slowly stir the mixture with a wooden spoon until it thickens, being careful not to incorporate any air into the mix. Once it is thick enough to coat the back of the spoon, remove from the heat and pour immediately into 10 small ramekins, filling them to about 5 mm from the rim.

Place the ramekins in a *bain-marie* and put into a 140 °C oven for about 40 minutes, or until set. (Check by gently shaking the ramekins – there should be a slight wobble towards the centre.)

Remove the ramekins from the *bain-marie* and allow to cool. Place in the fridge overnight.

About an hour before serving, remove from the fridge. When you are ready to serve, sprinkle with muscovado sugar and use a blowtorch to caramelise.

MARKUS FARBINGER & LIEZIE MULDER

Tuscan white bean salsa
Fresh summer vegetable salad
Roman pizza Margherita
Steamed mussels & Butterflied LM prawns
Spiced coffee granita with vanilla cream

Ask anybody in the industry and they'll tell you how tough running a restaurant is. They'll throw out words like "recession" and go on about how demanding winter months can be. And they're right.

Nobody bothered to tell Markus Farbinger and Liezie Mulder – the owners of Ile de Pain in Knysna. Their humble café is consistently heaving. Queues are standard. In season people line up around the block to get in. Sometimes they're there before the place has even opened its doors. The best part? Take a look at those faces in the queue. Nobody seems to mind at all. In fact, they all seem excited to get in there and start eating. This is because most of them are returning, not visiting for the first time. In other words, they've tasted this food before. And I hate even calling it food, because it's so much more than that.

A colossal, traditional stone oven takes centre stage at Ile de Pain. Every day, with the sun not yet making an appearance, the IDP team rise and start their work. For them, baking is about more than the incredible breads they produce. Sure, they happen to be the best in the country, but it's about a way of life too. With a ritualistic – almost monastic – approach, there are no shortcuts. Everything is done by hand, everything is done by feel and everything is kept as close to its most natural state as possible. Bread from this place has the ability to nourish, to heal, to spark a smile and to bring a halt to a bad day.

The style of food the rest of the menu offers is deceptively simple, the type of food Liezie and Markus eat every day at home.

The day we spend cooking with the two of them is a story of contrasts. With their house only a few steps away, Markus invites us into the restaurant kitchen to knock up a "Roman" pizza, so named because he saw something similar on one of his travels. (IDP does so well that he and Liezie pack up and travel every year, searching for new ideas and inspiration.) The end result is a metre-long pizza, dressed simply with mozzarella, fresh and cooked tomatoes and basil leaves. We talk in the kitchen, which is absolutely still. It's almost therapeutic. The pizza is loaded onto a custom-made board and carried down to the house, where the scene is slightly different …

Liezie has taken over the next few dishes. With her sister acting as her trusty sous chef, and every single guest crammed into the tiny kitchen, they are frying off heaps of butterflied prawns and piles of mussels. The music is loud, wine glasses are full and the beer is cold. A vegetable salad kicks off the feast, while a sharp grappa and an indulgent dessert ends it. Somewhere in between, those prawns and mussels are obliterated.

This party is warming up, but we've got to get going. We will be driving back to Cape Town the following day, and I need to factor in having breakfast at IDP. Stop judging me – it's on the way. I'd stop even if it wasn't.

TUSCAN WHITE BEAN SALSA

SERVES 4 – 6 AS A PRE-LUNCH SNACK

- 1 can (400 g) cannellini beans, drained
- ½ can (200 g) chickpeas, drained
- 2 teaspoons minced garlic
- ½ teaspoon ground cumin
- 1 ½ tablespoons finely chopped red onion
- 1 ½ tablespoons finely chopped parsley
- 3 tablespoons olive oil
- 1 ½ tablespoons lemon juice

Combine all the ingredients in a food processor, and pulse until the desired consistency is reached.

Scoop into a bowl, drizzle with olive oil and balsamic vinegar, and serve with good, fresh bread or your favourite savoury biscuits.

CHEF'S NOTE: I prefer the salsa to be slightly chunky, so when I combine all the ingredients, I keep aside a third of the mix to blend in by hand at the end.

FRESH SUMMER VEGETABLE SALAD

SERVES 6

THE VINAIGRETTE
- 1 tablespoon Dijon mustard
- 1 tablespoon honey
- 2 tablespoons orange juice
- 125 ml red wine vinegar
- 250 ml olive oil
- 2 tablespoons chopped parsley
- 1 tablespoon chopped coriander
- salt and pepper, to taste

THE SALAD
- 2 bunches asparagus
- 2 medium fennel bulbs
- 8 courgettes
- 1 red pepper, deseeded
- 2 oranges, segmented

Whisk the mustard, honey, orange juice and red wine vinegar together. Whisk in the olive oil in a steady stream until well incorporated. Throw in the herbs, and flavour with salt and pepper. Set aside till required.

To make the salad, trim the ends off the asparagus and blanch for 1 to 2 minutes; there should still be a bite to it.

Shave the fennel bulbs very thinly on a mandolin slicer. (Use a sharp knife to cut as thinly as possible if you don't have a mandolin.) Likewise, shave or cut the courgettes lengthwise into long, thin ribbons.

Slice the red pepper into very thin strips. Cut away the peel and the pith of both oranges. Hold the orange in the palm of your hand and run a sharp knife along the membrane of each segment to loosen and remove them.

To serve, arrange on a serving platter and pour most of the dressing over the salad. Use your hands to toss, ensuring that everything is well coated. Pour the remaining dressing in a small bowl and serve on the table.

ROMAN PIZZA MARGHERITA

SERVES 6 AS A STARTER

- 400 g bread dough (see recipe on page 163)
- 80 g quickly blanched and peeled tomatoes, left whole
- 80 g tinned tomatoes (only use the very best Italian tinned tomatoes)
- 160 g *fior di latte* mozzarella (the finest you can find)
- 10 fresh basil leaves
- olive oil, to taste
- salt, pepper, sugar and lemon juice, to taste

Preheat the oven to 250 °C. (You will need something to put at the bottom of the oven to retain heat and cook the bottom of the pizza. A baker's stone is ideal but a heat-proof tile works too.) Allow the oven to warm up for 45 minutes.

Meanwhile, stretch the dough onto a floured surface and roll into a rectangle, roughly 400 mm x 200 mm. The edges should be slightly thicker than the middle.

Mix all the tomatoes gently with a spoon to ensure the whole tomatoes don't lose their texture. Place the dough carefully on a board lined with baking paper and roughly spread the tomato topping onto the dough. You want it to be rustic and uneven.

Tear your mozzarella into pieces and scatter on top of the pizza. Finish by placing the basil leaves onto the sauce amongst the mozzarella pieces. Make sure the leaves are pressed into the sauce to ensure that they do not burn in the oven.

Finally drizzle the pizza with the olive oil and season with a sprinkling of sugar, some lemon juice, salt and pepper.

Gently slide the pizza onto the preheated baking surface and cook for 5 to 7 minutes, or until the edges are nicely bubbled and charred. Remove, allow to cool for a minute on a rack, and cut into whatever portions you want.

TIP: Never cut mozzarella of this quality. If you do, you will lose the beautifully fragrant "milk". Plus it will make your pizza base soggy.

STEAMED MUSSELS

SERVES 6

- 1 kg fresh mussels
- 1 onion, finely diced
- olive oil
- 2 cloves garlic, finely chopped
- 250 ml white wine
- 1 cup fish stock
- 125 ml cream
- juice of 1 lemon
- 1 tablespoon fish sauce
- 1 bunch parsley, roughly chopped

Clean and de-beard the mussels, discarding any that are open. Sauté the onion with a little olive oil in a deep pot for about 6 to 7 minutes, or until translucent. Add the garlic and sauté for another 2 minutes.

Throw all the cleaned mussels into the pot, along with the wine, and cook covered for 2 to 3 minutes, or until the mussels are open. Using a slotted spoon, transfer them to a large bowl, discarding any that have failed to open.

Pour your stock into the pot and simmer on medium heat, until the liquid is reduced by about a third. Add the cream, lemon juice, fish sauce and parsley and heat through. Pour the hot broth over the mussels.

Serve in a large bowl set in the middle of the table, or as individually plated portions. Serve with a crusty baguette to mop up all the juices.

BUTTERFLIED LM PRAWNS

WITH MUSTARD BUTTER | SERVES 6

THE MUSTARD BUTTER
- 500 g soft unsalted butter
- 175 ml lemon juice
- 2 tablespoons Pernod
- 1 tablespoon Tabasco sauce
- 2 tablespoons Dijon mustard

Melt all the ingredients for the mustard butter in a small saucepan. Let it come up to a boil, reduce the heat and keep warm.

THE PRAWNS
- 36 – 40 queen LM prawns, deveined and butterflied
- clarified butter, as needed
- salt and pepper, to taste
- mustard butter, as needed
- ½ bunch parsley, roughly chopped

In a large frying pan, or flat-top griddle, sauté the prawns flesh-side down in a little clarified butter over medium heat.

As soon as the prawn shells start turning pink, flip them over and cook the shell-side until crispy (be careful not to overcook). Season to taste. Keep warm in a low oven until all the prawns are cooked.

Just before serving, drizzle the crispy prawns with mustard butter and sprinkle over the chopped parsley. Serve as finger food or with steamed jasmine rice as a main course.

Don't be tempted to overcook the mussels and the prawns – they will become rubbery. This is a common mistake among home cooks.

SPICED COFFEE GRANITA

WITH VANILLA CREAM | SERVES 8 – 10

SPICY SYRUP

– 200 g sugar
– 125 ml water
– 1 cinnamon stick
– zest from 1 lemon
– ½ piece star anise

To make the syrup, bring the sugar, water and spices to a brief simmer. Do not boil, but allow the sauce to thicken and the sugar to dissolve.

When ready, remove from the heat and cool. Store covered in the refrigerator and use when required. This is also great with homemade iced tea or lemonade.

THE GRANITA

– 500 ml strong, good
  espresso, cooled
– 125 ml spicy syrup

Mix the espresso and syrup, and pour into a freezer-proof container. Freeze for 30 minutes, whisk the mixture, and return to the freezer. Repeat every 30 minutes until dry crystals form. Freeze overnight. Whisk into fine crystals just before serving.

VANILLA CREAM

– 420 ml cream
– 22 g icing sugar
– seeds from ½ vanilla pod

To make the vanilla cream, simply whip the cream, sugar and vanilla until soft peaks form. Keep in the fridge until needed.

To assemble the dessert, chill suitable serving glasses in advance and fill them ¾ of the way with the granita. Top with the vanilla cream. This is magic served with good grappa on the side and something crunchy like your favourite biscuit, or a sugar cigar.

NOTE: This recipe must be made a day or even several days in advance to avoid stress. This sounds like a lot of effort or planning, however once the granita is made it can be stored for several days in the freezer in a closed container.

KAREN DUDLEY

Appleteria
Creamy scrambled eggs
Spend-the-night tomatoes
Honey-mustard sausages

Having lived in the area for almost a decade, Karen Dudley is pretty familiar with Woodstock and the "revival" that has become a popular word among property developers in recent times. She was there long before the area became trendy for young couples, advertising agencies and boutique furniture stores. She was there to see the flurry of restaurants, hotels, studio apartments, galleries and Cape Town's most successful food market. And, having run her catering company from her home kitchen for years, she was (maybe without knowing it) playing a major part in the process, just through her refusal to go anywhere else.

Nothing symbolises change like a physical space though, and her decision to move her swelling business into a shop in Main Road was further evidence of her faith in the suburb. Taking over an old fishery (which apparently smelled as bad as you'd expect), she opened her new premises, with a small café attached. Simply named The Kitchen, Karen's restaurant is one of the coolest in the city.

Imagine putting all the characters and colours of Alice in Wonderland into a blender and then taking the resulting mix and kind of just throwing it around a room. That's the vibe at The Kitchen. The place is dripping with a vibrant energy that you can't buy or recreate. It's a special, intangible quality that some have and others don't. It's the X-Factor. Karen Dudley has it. The Kitchen has it. So, when we pull into Karen's place, I'm intrigued to see if her house is as brilliantly eclectic as her restaurant. It's not. It's better. Karen is like our very own Frida Kahlo, and her house is a kaleidoscope of colours, jam-packed with a lifetime of trinkets.

Karen arrives at the same time as we do. She had "popped out" to buy some fresh koeksisters from her neighbour, who makes them herself. "You didn't think I was going to do all the cooking, did you?" she laughs. Still warm, the dough is laced with cardamom and coconut. They're light instead of oily, beautifully balanced in flavour instead of sickly sweet. You could throw these things in the air and they might never land. They're unforgettable.

Having invited us for breakfast she then lovingly serves up plates *heaving* with silky scrambled eggs, giant sausages and tomatoes that she has roasted through the night. Artisan coffee is roasted and chai tea is poured. The OJ is so fresh you can't drink it through a straw. The kids are playing and laughing and so are the guests – it's a quintessential lazy Sunday.

Karen Dudley is an amazing woman and her ability to take something seemingly plain and inject so much personality into it is the hallmark of her cooking. I ask her if she thinks that's why Michelle Obama squeezed in a quick lunch at her place earlier that month. She laughs it off, "I do honest food. Maybe she just felt like a sandwich made with love."

We head outside to find my car window smashed. Karen is more devastated than me. Typically, she's quick to defend her beloved Woodstock, and insists that it never happens anymore. She is that kind of woman. I don't really care; I've got some of those koeksisters in my bag anyway.

89

APPLETERIA

SERVES 1

- 250 ml good Greek yoghurt
- 1 large Granny Smith apple, partly peeled and grated
- 1 tablespoon cinnamon sugar
- 2 tablespoons runny honey
- 5 toasted almonds or hazelnuts, roughly chopped
- 3 pitted dates, roughly chopped
- 2 tablespoons of your favourite granola (optional)

Scoop the yoghurt into a mound in a bowl. Pile the grated apple on top. Sprinkle on the cinnamon sugar (you can make it in advance by mixing equal parts of ground cinnamon and sugar) and drizzle with honey. Finish off with the other bits.

CHEF'S NOTE: Goodness knows how I came on the name for this breakfast confection! It makes people very happy. Don't be shy with the cinnamon sugar.

CREAMY SCRAMBLED EGGS

SERVES 1

- **2 organic eggs**
- **3 tablespoons fresh cream**
- **pinch of Maldon salt**
- **1 teaspoon white pepper**
- **½ teaspoon freshly grated nutmeg**
- **½ tablespoon butter**

Thoroughly whisk the eggs, cream and seasoning in a small bowl.

Heat a non-stick pan over medium heat and add the butter. Pour in the egg mixture. Consider yourself a Buddhist monk in a garden and, using a wide, flexible rubber spatula, ever-so-calmly move your eggs gently around the pan. You want folded eggs, rather than messy dry ones.

Take your time. Go slowly with your spatula around the edges and in the same direction. When the eggs are just set, slip them onto warm, buttered toast.

CHEF'S NOTE: Everything I know about eggs, I learnt from my Sweetheart. I am a fast and furious and passionate cook. My husband is steady, careful and gentle. Eggs require that you hold back your power.

SPEND-THE-NIGHT TOMATOES

SERVES 4

- 8 small tomatoes
  (2 per person)
- olive oil
- 4 teaspoons sugar
- sea salt
- 4 teaspoons dried thyme

Preheat the oven to its highest temperature. Cut the tomatoes in half and toss with the olive oil, sugar, salt and thyme, and lay on a baking tray lined with baking paper.

Blast-roast the tomatoes for 7 minutes and then turn the oven off. (Do not be tempted to open the oven door to see what the tomatoes are doing.)

Leave them in privacy. And see the next morning that they have become the essence of roasted tomato.

Serve with creamy scrambled eggs (see recipe on page 93).

HONEY-MUSTARD SAUSAGES

MAKE AS MANY AS YOU LIKE

- 1 to 2 top-quality pork bangers
  per person
- equal parts grainy mustard
  and honey

Line a baking tray with baking paper. Pour on a drizzle of vegetable oil.

Line up the sausages in ranks. Smother with the honey mustard mixture.

Bake in a preheated oven at 190 °C for 25 to 35 minutes. You may need to turn them halfway through cooking and baste with the honey-mustard glaze to ensure even and perfect colour.

Serve with creamy scrambled eggs (see recipe on page 93).

Dear Carol
Thanks for
the support
Weskus groete

KOBUS VAN DER MERWE

Deboned leg of springbok on the braai with Marinated mushrooms
Angelfish bobotie with Apple and cabbage sambal
Sweetcorn ice cream with tomato jam and shortbread crumbs

We've all had those moments, haven't we? Those days that leave you wanting to pack up your desk, move out of the city and start a job that you love instead of one that merely pays the bills. The difference with Kobus van der Merwe is that he actually went and did it.

Leaving a position as online editor for a leading food publication, Kobus was always going to remain in the industry. Somehow. But sitting in front of a computer all day was strangling him. Instead, Kobus left the city and headed for the sleepy West Coast town of Paternoster, where his folks were running a tiny café/deli/shop called Oep ve Koep. Kobus moved in, opened Oep ve Koep Bistro (the restaurant element of the store) and hasn't looked back.

Getting his hands on fresh ingredients out there proved to be a bit challenging, so Kobus began foraging for his own. He now trawls the dunes looking for edible herbs and plants, most of which people have never heard of. He doesn't buy cheese, he makes his own. Cured meats? He does that himself. Sausages? Handmade in the kitchen. Breads? Don't bother delivering them.

This is food made from scratch, as our ancestors would've wanted. But – and this is a big but – the food that Kobus prepares in that matchbox of a kitchen must rate as some of the most exciting I've seen. Not only in South Africa. The guy is a genius; quite simply, one of the most creative chefs I've ever seen.

Paternoster is putting on quite a show for us when we pull in. In fact, she's flat-out showing off. With crackerjack views of bone-white beaches and blue sea, a table has been prepared on the balcony. It's rustic, beautiful and weathered, bearing reminders of (I'm guessing) plenty of boozy lunches.

Kobus's family helps out throughout the day. Mom is in and out of the kitchen (despite Kobus *ordering* her to relax). Sister is in charge of drinks. Dad is manning some slabs of springbok in a smoky Weber. And Kobus manages to throw out plenty of food, seemingly without any effort.

A South African classic, bobotie, is given the West Coast treatment and prepared with angelfish instead of the traditional lamb or beef. The springbok is expertly cooked and served with crunchy greens, including some trademark local dune spinach. It's vintage Kobus van der Merwe and, even though he's toned it down a bit, his quirkiness shines through with every bite.

He's saved the best for last. An unusual corn ice cream is offered up with tomato jam. Crunchy, homemade shortbread crumbs add some texture. It belongs in a fine-dining restaurant.

The atmosphere out there is – as you'd expect – pretty chilled. It washes over you, and everyday troubles seem far away. None of Kobus's Cape Town guests seem too bothered about leaving; they look like a troop plucked from the latest American Apparel catalogue as they sip bubbly and talk of a stroll on the beach to allow the food to settle.

I think Kobus is onto something here.

DEBONED LEG OF SPRINGBOK

ON THE BRAAI | SERVES 10 – 12

– 1 deboned leg of springbok
– 5 cloves garlic, roughly chopped
– juice of 1 lemon
– 4 tablespoons olive oil
– black pepper
– salt

Lightly score the meat with a sharp boning knife. Mix the chopped garlic, lemon juice and olive oil, and massage it into the meat. Leave to marinate, preferably overnight.

Season the meat and cook it on a kettle braai (Weber) over hot coals, indirect method, for 30 to 35 minutes, or until medium rare (if you have a meat thermometer the core temperature should be at approximately 50 °C).

Allow to rest for 10 minutes before carving. Serve with some marinated mushrooms, roasted tomato and stir-fried courgette, mange tout and young dune spinach shoots. (You can substitute with baby spinach here).

MARINATED MUSHROOMS

SERVES 6 AS A SIDE DISH

– 4 tablespoons olive oil
– 2 tablespoons soy sauce
– 2 tablespoons balsamic vinegar
– 1 teaspoon *moskonfyt*
– handful each of button, oyster, and pine oyster mushrooms, finely sliced
– black pepper

Combine the olive oil, soy sauce, balsamic vinegar and *moskonfyt*. Pour over the finely sliced mushrooms and stir through. Add freshly ground black pepper to taste.

Set aside for at least an hour to allow the flavours to mature and the mushrooms to absorb the marinade.

Serve as a side dish with the springbok.

It's vintage Kobus van der Merwe and, even though he's toned it down a bit, his quirkiness shines through with every bite.

ANGELFISH BOBOTIE

SERVES 10

- 8 medium-sized angelfish fillets
- olive oil, for frying
- salt and pepper, to taste
- 1 large onion, chopped
- 2 small fennel bulbs, finely chopped
- 5 cloves garlic, crushed
- 10 cm stem ginger, finely sliced
- 4 tablespoons masala
- 2 teaspoons ground turmeric
- 400 g cooked lentils
- 4 tablespoons balsamic vinegar
- 4 tablespoons apricot jam
- dash of soy sauce
- dash of fish sauce
- 3 eggs
- 125 ml buttermilk
- 1 teaspoon ground turmeric, for the custard

Pan-fry the angelfish fillets in a little olive oil until just cooked, seasoning with salt and pepper as you go. Allow to cool slightly, then use your hands to flake the fish into small pieces.

Fry the onion, fennel, garlic, ginger and spices in olive oil until fragrant. Add the flaked angelfish and cooked lentils, and stir through.

Next add the balsamic vinegar, apricot jam, soy sauce and fish sauce, and mix so that everything is combined. Taste for sweet-sour balance and adjust if necessary.

Spoon the mixture into a greased, oven-proof dish, pressing down gently and smoothing the top with the back of a spoon.

Lightly beat the eggs, buttermilk and turmeric powder together. Gently pour the custard over the angelfish mixture. Bake at 150 °C for approximately 30 minutes, or until lightly browned.

Serve with some apple and cabbage sambal, a tangy peach chutney and full cream yoghurt as accompaniments.

APPLE AND CABBAGE SAMBAL

MAKES 10 PORTIONS

- 2 Granny Smith apples, very finely sliced
- small red cabbage, shredded
- 1 cup chopped fresh coriander
- juice of ½ lemon

Mix the chopped apple and cabbage with the coriander. Finish by squeezing over the lemon juice. Serve as an accompaniment to the bobotie.

SWEETCORN ICE CREAM

WITH TOMATO JAM AND SHORTBREAD CRUMBS | SERVES 8 – 10

THE ICE CREAM

- 4 whole cobs of sweetcorn
- 1 litre full cream milk
- 200 g sugar
- 8 egg yolks
- 200 ml cream

Slice the kernels off the sweetcorn cobs and reserve the husks. Blend the kernels into a paste using a food processor. Refrigerate until required.

Combine the milk, sugar and sweetcorn husks in a large saucepan, and bring to a boil. Simmer gently for a short while to allow the flavour of the husks to infuse the mixture. Remove the husks and discard.

Beat the egg yolks to ribbon stage. Pour the hot milk onto the egg yolk mixture and whisk through. Return to the saucepan and cook until slightly thickened. Remove from the heat, pour into a chilled metal bowl and refrigerate overnight.

Combine the chilled custard mixture with the cream and sweetcorn purée. Strain and churn in an ice-cream maker.

When the ice cream is ready, serve with shortbread crumbs, fresh baby corn slices and a sticky, sweet tomato jam.

THE SHORTBREAD CRUMBS

- 200 g cake flour
- 200 g butter
- 100 g castor sugar
- pinch of salt

Place all the ingredients in a food processor and blend until it just comes together.

Press into a pastry tin, pierce with a fork and bake at 180 °C until golden brown.

Allow to cool, then break into crumbs. Serve with the sweetcorn ice cream.

LIAM TOMLIN

Mezze trio of Hummus, Spiced aubergine and Raclette
Singapore chicken with rice
Chocolate fondant

Liam Tomlin is the only chef in this book who isn't currently working in a restaurant. So, why was I willing to make an exception? Consider these points and then you tell me. When he worked in Australia he was voted chef of the year in 2001. In the same year his restaurant, BANC, was voted restaurant of the year. He's worked alongside cooking greats like Michel Roux. He's got a couple of his own books, and is currently working on a new one. It should be obvious why.

Nowadays Liam runs Chef's Warehouse, a cookery school and high-end kitchen equipment shop in town. With jaw-droppingly beautiful equipment and the best cookbook collection in the country, it's the kind of place you don't want to find yourself in on payday. At the time of writing Liam was putting finishing touches to the second Chef's Warehouse – a culinary playground on the Leopard's Leap wine estate in Franschhoek. There's little doubt it will be a massive success.

From the impeccable, hand-selected kit in the shop, we already know Liam's a stylish cat, and when we are let into his loft penthouse in the middle of town, that's confirmed. His wife Jan waves her hand over a beautiful table and says they were supposed to take delivery of one much bigger that morning. "We've got way too many people now, and I've got no idea where everybody's going to eat." If she's really worried, she's doing a good job of hiding it. Making sure the bubbly is on ice seems to be a priority and we are told to make ourselves at home. Straight off

the bat I know that this is the type of lunch where you are encouraged to simply relax.

Their place is beautiful. A massive contemporary art piece is the main feature and windows frame a spectacular view of Table Mountain, but it's Liam's collection of cookbooks that draws me in. Hands-down the best I've seen. Displayed as beautifully as in the shop, it's an incredible collection.

Within an hour the apartment is humming with activity. Guests prefer to cram into the kitchen than to sit at a table or on a couch, and Liam and Jan are throwing food down onto an impromptu buffet table. "This is real food, man," smiles Liam. He's loving it and explains that simple food is his favourite when it's done properly. And trust me, this is done properly.

A raclette is scooped onto crusty bread and served with spaetzle laced with asparagus tips. A chicken is slow-poached in a delicate broth with hints of sesame oil, ginger, garlic, lemon grass and chilli. Even his rice tastes ridiculous, the addition of soya sauce and some spring onions being enough to make it more than an afterthought. Gooey chocolate fondants round off the meal.

Somewhere in between bites of this feast, Liam states defiantly that food is getting too complicated. "Food always tastes better when eaten with loved ones, doesn't it? Why are there so many 'critics' out there nowadays? You should enjoy a meal, not try and explain what the chef has done wrong."

"For sure," I agree. Besides, I couldn't find much wrong with the chef's food on the day anyway.

MEZZE TRIO

OF HUMMUS, SPICED AUBERGINE AND RACLETTE | SERVES 8

HUMMUS

- 400 g cooked chickpeas
- 5 tablespoons hot water
- 125 g tahini
- 5 tablespoons extra virgin olive oil
- juice of 1 lemon
- 3 cloves garlic, peeled and chopped
- 1 teaspoon ground cumin
- salt, to taste
- black pepper, freshly ground
- pinch of paprika

Place the chickpeas, water, tahini, olive oil and half the lemon juice into a food blender, and mix until smooth.

Add the garlic, cumin, salt and freshly ground pepper. Taste and adjust the seasoning if necessary.

Spoon into a serving bowl and drizzle with a thin layer of olive oil. Sprinkle with paprika just before serving.

Serve with fresh, crusty bread. Makes enough for 8 as part of a mezze platter.

SPICED AUBERGINE

- 3 large aubergines
- 2 cloves garlic, peeled and sliced
- 2 bay leaves
- 4 sprigs fresh thyme
- 2 tablespoons tomato purée
- 1 tablespoon mild curry powder
- 5 teaspoons ground cumin
- salt and pepper
- 4 tablespoons olive oil
- small bunch coriander

Heat the oven to 180 °C. Cut the aubergines in half lengthways and, using the tip of a knife, make deep incisions in a small diamond pattern in the flesh. (Don't cut through the skin). Push the garlic, bay leaves and thyme into the incisions and spread the tomato purée over the top. Sprinkle with the spices and season with salt and pepper.

Drizzle with olive oil and sandwich the halves back together. Wrap tightly in foil and roast on a baking tray for an hour, or until soft.

Unwrap the aubergines and, using a spoon, scrape out the flesh into a sieve suspended over a bowl. Pick out the bay leaves and thyme and allow the flesh to drain for about an hour.

Transfer to a chopping board and chop roughly. Heat a frying pan and cook the aubergine over a medium heat until it takes on some colour and looks dry. Add coriander as a garnish and serve with chunky bread as part of a mezze platter.

(See page 112 for Raclette recipe.)

MEZZE TRIO

OF HUMMUS, SPICED AUBERGINE AND RACLETTE | SERVES 8

RACLETTE
- ½ a wheel of raclette cheese (usually about 2 – 3 kg)
- baguettes (or your favourite bread)

Light a fire and while it gets going, scrape off the rind of the cheese on the top and the bottom. When the fire dies down to glowing coals, place a heat-proof stone or tile near the heat. Place the cheese onto the stone, with the cut surface exposed to the fire. As the cheese melts, scrape it off onto your bread.

Serve with a variety of cold meats, gherkins and pickled onions. Serves 8 as part of a mezze platter.

(See page 111 for Hummus and Spiced aubergine recipes.)

SINGAPORE CHICKEN

WITH RICE | SERVES 6 – 8

CHINESE SPICE SALT

- 2 tablespoons sea salt
- 1 teaspoon Szechuan peppercorns
- 2 teaspoons Chinese five-spice powder

Place the salt and peppercorns in a bowl and mix together. Dry-roast over a gentle heat until fragrant.

Remove, cool and grind to a fine powder. Pass through a fine sieve, discarding any husks. Refrigerate until ready to use. Mix through the five-spice powder just before serving.

TOGARASHI DRESSING

- 2 teaspoons peeled and finely chopped ginger
- 1 teaspoon finely chopped garlic
- 2 red chillies, seeded and finely chopped
- 1½ tablespoons sesame oil
- 2 tablespoons peanut oil
- juice of 1 fresh lime
- 1½ tablespoons soya sauce
- 1 teaspoon sugar
- 2 teaspoons hot chilli powder

Mix all the ingredients for the dressing together well. Set aside, allowing the flavours to develop, until you are ready to serve.

THE CHICKEN

- 1 whole free-range chicken
- 3 litres chicken stock
- 3 cloves garlic
- 2 finger-sized pieces of fresh ginger, peeled
- 2 whole spring onions
- 6 whole white peppercorns, crushed
- ½ teaspoon salt
- 2 tablespoons sesame oil

To prepare the chicken, wash it thoroughly and put it in a heavy-based pot. Cover with the chicken stock, and add the garlic, ginger, spring onion, peppercorns and salt. With the heat at a simmer (not boiling) cook the chicken for 45 minutes. Turn the heat off and leave the chicken in the stock for a further 15 minutes. Test a thigh with a skewer – if the juices run pale pink it's cooked.

Remove the chicken from the pot with a slotted spoon and set aside to cool for 10 minutes. Rub the chicken all over with sesame oil and remove the legs and breasts from the bone. Slice into even pieces, and set aside until ready to serve.

THE RICE

- 3 tablespoons vegetable oil
- 1 tablespoon sesame oil
- 2 shallots, finely chopped
- 5 cloves garlic, peeled and finely chopped
- 1 finger-sized piece of fresh ginger, peeled and chopped
- 400 g long-grain rice
- 600 ml chicken stock (from the poached chicken)
- a pinch of salt
- 1 small bunch coriander (for garnish)
- 1 cup spring onion, finely sliced (for garnish)

While the chicken is cooking, get started on the rice. Heat the vegetable oil and sesame oil together in a large pan over medium heat. Sauté the shallots, garlic and ginger until fragrant, making sure not to get any colour on them.

Rinse and drain the rice. Add it to the pot and stir until evenly coated. Pour in the chicken stock (from the poached chicken) and season with a pinch of salt.

Bring to the boil, cover and reduce heat to low. Simmer for 15 to 20 minutes, or until you can see "steam holes" appearing on the surface of the rice.

To assemble the dish, spoon the rice onto a serving platter and arrange the chicken slices on top. Garnish with coriander and sliced spring onion. Serve with a bowl of the togarashi dressing and a small dish of the Chinese spice salt on the side.

CHOCOLATE FONDANT

SERVES 8

- 20 g melted, unsalted butter (for lining moulds)
- castor sugar (for lining moulds)
- 200 g good-quality dark chocolate, finely chopped
- 200 g softened, unsalted butter
- 200 g icing sugar, sifted, plus extra for dusting
- 4 medium-sized free-range eggs
- 4 medium-sized free-range egg yolks
- 55 g plain flour
- 35 g good-quality cocoa powder
- toasted almond flakes (for garnish)

Preheat oven to 190 °C. Prepare 8 moulds or ramekins by brushing them with softened butter, using upwards strokes. Chill until firm then brush them again with another layer of butter. Coat the ramekins with castor sugar, shaking off any excess. Place the ramekins onto a baking tray and set aside.

Put the chocolate into a stainless steel bowl and set over a pot of simmering water. Stir the chocolate until melted and smooth. Keep warm.

Using an electric mixer, cream the butter and icing sugar together until pale and doubled in volume. Mix the whole eggs and egg yolks together and add them a little at a time to the creamed butter and sugar, beating well between each addition. Reduce the speed of the mixer and add the melted chocolate.

Remove the bowl from the mixer and sift in the flour and cocoa powder, folding as you go. (Be careful not to overwork the mixture.) Spoon the mixture into the prepared ramekins, filling them to just past halfway. Place in the oven and bake for 8 to 10 minutes.

After 8 minutes, remove one of the fondants and check it with a skewer. It should be cooked around the edges but the centre needs to be liquid. The skewer should come away easily though – if it doesn't, return the fondants to the oven for another 2 minutes.

Remove when done and allow to rest for 1 minute, before carefully turning each one onto your chosen serving plates. Dust with icing sugar and serve with a scattering of toasted almond flakes.

LUKE DALE-ROBERTS

Slow-roasted Asian pork belly with black bean salsa
Roasted aubergine and feta dip
Whole Cape salmon, with roasted tomato, herbs and chickpea broth

You'd be hard-pressed to find a local chef in hotter demand. Luke Dale-Roberts is a culinary genius. And, like anyone who truly deserves to be called that, he'd probably hate it. Having spearheaded La Colombe to the lofty heights of 12th best restaurant in the world in 2010 (according to the annual San Pellegrino World's 50 Best Restaurants list), his new spot, The Test Kitchen, is a tiny industrial space in Woodstock's creative hub, The Old Biscuit Mill. It's quite a departure from the cushy vineyards of Constantia. It's a little bit edgier. A little bit younger. A little bit more fun. And it's the hottest ticket in town.

The food is phenomenal, and to maintain the impeccable standards, Luke works like a karaoke repairman in Japan. In fact, when I call him up to try and nail down some possible dates, he laughs and jokes that he spends more time with his kitchen staff than with his friends and family. I laugh too. Then we both stop and – in a moment of clarity – realise that he's probably right. "So should we just do it here then?" Luke suggests. And so we do.

I arrive and Luke has already got his wood-burning oven on the go. It's situated in a courtyard outside his front door, and what follows is a feast, cooked pretty much exclusively out there. There are a few nervous moments, as Luke ducks into the kitchen to check his sauces (and, of course, to try and run his restaurant, which he and his staff are simultaneously prepping for dinner service). Every time he does that he asks me – far too nonchalantly I might add – to "make sure everything's cool and nothing gets burnt". Sure Luke. No pressure.

Fighting off images of a fish sliding into the flames, or a pork belly ending up on the floor, I poke around a bit but manage to avoid ruining anything. The meat is cooked perfectly. While I'm out there at least 10 people from surrounding offices come over and tell me that the food smells amazing. It does, of course, and I take great care in pretending it's my work in there.

When everything is done, Luke doesn't bother setting a table. Instead he cracks open a few bottles of wine and sits with his staff at bar counters inside. There they help themselves, buffet style, to a belting lunch. There's a feeling of mutual respect between head chef and crew. No airs and graces here. There's no ego and no arrogance from the man who has often been applauded as the best chef in the country. Instead he sits, eats and laughs side by side with his staff and me. These guys and girls are the people that he works with in the trenches every day. When lunch is done, they wipe down the surfaces as a team.

It's time to push on. There's a waiting list for dinner that night and, having got to enjoy lunch with the team, I'm not surprised. They're doing awesome things in that place. Besides, there's a waiting list every night.

SLOW-ROASTED ASIAN PORK BELLY

WITH BLACK BEAN SALSA | SERVES 8

THE PORK BELLY

- 125 ml Chinese five-spice mixture
- 500 ml rock salt
- 125 ml sugar
- zest of 1 orange
- 1.5 kg pork belly
- crushed peanuts
- shredded spring onions

Preheat your oven to 220 °C. (Or get your braai coals nice and hot.) Using a pestle and mortar pound the five-spice powder, salt, sugar and orange zest together until you've got a rough paste.

Score the skin of the belly and rub the spice mixture into the meat. Brush off any excess, turn the meat over and rub more of the spice into the other side. Roast the belly skin-side up for 30 minutes, then reduce the heat to 180 °C and cook for another 2 hours, or until the skin is crispy and the meat flakes easily.

If cooking on the braai, push the wood or coals to the side and cook slowly over indirect heat for about 3 hours, making sure that you add coals to keep the temperature consistent throughout the cooking period.

Remove from the heat and leave to rest for a few minutes. Serve warm drizzled with black bean salsa on wilted Asian greens. Garnish with the peanuts and spring onions.

THE BLACK BEAN SALSA

- 30 g peeled and finely chopped garlic
- 40 g peeled and chopped ginger
- 50 g chopped lemon grass
- 85 g chopped red onion
- 180 ml olive oil
- 2 tablespoons sesame oil
- 4 tablespoons brown sugar
- 200 ml sherry
- 125 g soaked black beans

Fry your garlic, ginger, lemon grass and onion in the olive oil for a few minutes.

Add the sesame oil, sugar and sherry, and bring to the boil. Reduce to a simmer and add the soaked beans.

Stir through until the flavours have come together, then remove from the heat and allow to cool.

When the pork is ready to serve, cut or tear the meat and pour the salsa over.

TIP: Crushed peanuts and shredded spring onions make simple garnishes that will give the dish a professional finish.

Some of these ingredients might sound exotic but you'd be surprised at how many supermarkets stock Asian flavours now. If you don't come right, check out speciality Asian shops in your area. Finding the right ingredients will make all the difference here.

ROASTED AUBERGINE AND FETA DIP

SERVES 4 – 6

- 2 aubergines
- 125 g feta cheese
- 50 g chopped pine nuts
- 2 tablespoons tahini
- 2 tablespoons white wine vinegar
- 150 ml olive oil

Roast the aubergines in an oven at 220 °C until blackened and soft. (If using the braai you can do this over indirect coals, but make sure they're very hot.)

Cut in half and scoop out the flesh. Blend everything until nicely emulsified. (Add some more oil if necessary.) Spread a thick layer on fresh bread as a snack, or serve as a rustic starter.

This dip can be stored in the fridge – use within 3 days.

WHOLE CAPE SALMON

WITH ROASTED TOMATO, HERBS AND CHICKPEA BROTH | SERVES 8

THE CAPE SALMON

- 1.5 kg whole Cape salmon, gutted and scaled
- sea salt and black pepper
- 20 g dill
- 10 g basil
- 1 lemon, sliced
- 150 ml olive oil

Slash the skin of the fish and season well. Scatter the herbs and lemon slices all over the fish (inside and out) and drizzle with olive oil. Braai the fish, or cook in an oven (at about 200 °C), until the flesh flakes easily.

NOTE: We've used Cape salmon here but there are a few fish that will work just as well. Just be sure to check out the SASSI list and use one from the green category.

THE CHICKPEA BROTH

- 250 g organic vine tomatoes
- 10–12 baby onions, halved
- salt and pepper
- 2 fennel bulbs, quartered
- 200 ml olive oil
- 6 cloves garlic, crushed
- 100 ml white wine
- 5 g fresh marjoram (or 1 teaspoon dried)
- 10 g fresh basil (plus extra for serving)
- 125 g cooked chickpeas
- balsamic vinegar
- 4 courgettes, cut into ribbons

Dice the tomatoes roughly. Put the onions and fennel on a tray, season with salt and pepper, and pour on some olive oil. Slow roast for about 30 minutes. (160 °C is a good temperature.) Remove and set aside.

Heat some more olive oil in a pan and add the garlic. Cook quickly until golden. Add the chopped tomatoes, white wine and all the herbs. Put the lid on, reduce the heat and cook for an hour.

When done, add the onions, fennel and chickpeas. Cook for a further 15 minutes, season to taste and add a drop or two of balsamic vinegar. Slice up extra basil as a garnish, along with the courgette ribbons.

MARGOT JANSE

Crayfish on the braai | Tomato and white anchovy salad
Baby gem salad with bacon and macadamia
Potato salad | Grilled courgettes and nectarines | Sorghum salad
Chocolate pavlova with passion fruit sabayon

It's an impossible task. Writing an introduction for a woman who needs no introduction. But I should just list the accolades Margot Janse has racked up since taking up her position as Executive Chef at Le Quartier Français Hotel in Franschhoek. Briefly.

The Tasting Room, Margot's fine-dining restaurant at the Hotel, has been ranked in the San Pellegrino World's 50 Best Restaurants list a staggering 8 times. It was named best restaurant in Africa and The Middle East by the same group no less than 5 times. Margot herself was awarded the position of Grand Chef by Relais & Châteaux in 2007, the same year taking home the trophy for Rising Chef of the Year.

So what makes her food so special? For me it's the storytelling she weaves into every dish. It's as much about why the ingredients are on the plate, as how they are prepared, which allows for a certain amount of theatre and nostalgia. So eating at The Tasting Room is a whole lot of fun (not always the case with fine dining). Most plates highlight a main ingredient but offset it with a combination that sticks in your mind long after you finish licking your plate. (Yes, you can do that there.)

Margot is like some kind of culinary sponge, and she often heads overseas to meet like-minded chefs and swap ideas and inspiration. She's a busy, busy woman and our day of shooting has been sandwiched in between two such trips.

It's a peach of a day. Having been given directions by a Franschhoek local (which I've learnt while writing this book never seem to include road names) we arrive late. "Drive up the hill, turn right at the grey house. You'll see a hedge. It's the last one on the right." As I step into the kitchen (late) I see a massive container filled with live crayfish. It should be a pretty decent lunch.

The day is one of those easy-going, make yourself at home, nobody cares how many beers you've had, we'll face tomorrow when it comes, kind of Sundays. The crayfish are humanely killed by Margot and cleaned by her husband, and fellow chef, Duncan. He's drawn the short straw for sure, but doesn't seem to notice. Pieter Ferreira (cellar master at Graham Beck wines) has brought along plenty of fizz and Duncan's full glass may have something to do with his good attitude. He proceeds to throw the spiny delicacies onto a massive fire, and within minutes they're done.

Outside, a long table groans under the weight of some belting food. Dense, sweet crayfish meat is washed down with bubbly and a bowl (quickly dubbed The Crayfish Graveyard) is passed around to offload empty shells. A selection of Margot's salads – stars in their own right – gets hoovered up.

The kids are in the pool when dessert arrives. They're having such a good time that they don't budge. No problem. More for the adults.

With more corks popping and people sinking deeper into the outdoor couches it's a lesson in self-restraint as we reluctantly leave. The day has been exactly what I had in mind when we started this book. And more.

133

CRAYFISH ON THE BRAAI

WITH LEMON BUTTER AND HOMEMADE AÏOLI | SERVES 10

THE CRAYFISH
- as many crayfish as you can eat, alive and kicking
- salt, to taste
- olive oil, to taste
- lemon juice, to taste

Cut the crayfish in half by very quickly sticking a sharp knife into the head, before cutting down the length of the tail. (If this is too hectic for you, ask your fishmonger to butterfly them.)

Wash them, pat dry and season with salt. Brush with olive oil and place cut-side down over the hot coals of a braai. Turn after 5 minutes and squeeze lemon juice over the cooked crayfish meat. Cook for a further minute or two, until only just done (do not overcook them).

Place your crayfish on a massive platter, or on individual plates, and serve with aïoli and lemon butter alongside.

TIP: Work on 1 to 1 ½ crayfish per person, but in all honesty get as many as you can eat.

THE LEMON BUTTER
- 125 ml lemon juice
- 50 ml cream
- 200 g butter, room temperature
- salt, to taste
- 1 tablespoon chopped chives

Reduce the lemon juice by half in a small pot and then add the cream. Reduce until halved once more. Take off the heat, and whisk in small pieces of butter, a little at a time. Season with salt and keep in a warm place.

Just before serving, add the chives and give it a final stir.

THE AÏOLI
- 1 head of garlic
- 3 high-quality, free-range egg yolks
- 2 tablespoons Dijon mustard
- 2 tablespoons white wine vinegar
- salt, to taste
- 100 ml olive oil
- 400 ml canola oil

Roast the head of garlic at 180 °C, until soft and caramelised. Cool and squeeze all the softened garlic out of the cloves.

Whisk the roasted garlic with the egg yolks, mustard, vinegar and salt until smooth. Mix the oils together and add drop by drop, whisking all the time. Continue this process until all the oil is incorporated.

TOMATO AND WHITE ANCHOVY SALAD

SERVES 10

- 1 kg Bella baby tomatoes
- 4 tablespoons extra virgin olive oil
- 4 teaspoons good balsamic vinegar
- salt and white pepper, to taste
- 200 g white pickled anchovies
- handful of basil leaves, torn

Bring a pot of water to the boil. Have a bowl of iced water ready. Blanch half the tomatoes in the boiling water for 30 seconds and place immediately in the iced water. Let the water come back to the boil and do the same with the rest.

Peel off the skins and add the tomatoes to a bowl, along with the olive oil and balsamic vinegar. Toss to make sure everything is well combined. Season with salt and white pepper, before adding the anchovy fillets and basil.

Give it all one final toss and serve in a bowl for everyone at the table to help themselves.

BABY GEM SALAD

WITH BACON AND MACADAMIA NUTS | SERVES 10

LIME AND YOLK DRESSING

- 2 high-quality, free-range egg yolks
- 3 tablespoons lime juice
- 1 small clove garlic, very finely chopped
- salt, to taste
- white pepper, to taste
- 300 ml olive oil

Whisk together the egg yolks, lime juice, garlic, and salt and pepper to taste.

Slowly add the oil, starting off drop by drop, and then moving to a thin, slow stream. Whisk continuously while doing this, until the oil is well incorporated. Set aside.

THE SALAD

- 300 g streaky bacon
- 5 baby gem lettuces, cut in half
- 1 cup roasted, salted macadamia nuts

Preheat the oven to 180 °C. Place the bacon in a roasting tray and cook until crispy. Leave to cool, before chopping into small pieces.

Place the baby gems in a bowl, cut-side up, and sprinkle with nuts and bacon. Finish with the lime and yolk dressing.

POTATO SALAD

SERVES 10

- 1 kg boiled baby potatoes, sliced
- 2 tablespoons olive oil
- 1 tablespoon crispy fried onion bits
- 1 tablespoon finely diced red onion
- 1 tablespoon finely diced sundried tomato
- smoked salt, to taste

Dress the sliced potatoes with the olive oil and sprinkle with the rest of the ingredients.

GRILLED COURGETTE

AND NECTARINE SALAD | SERVES 10

- 500 g courgettes (with flowers if possible), cut in half lengthways
- olive oil
- 3 nectarines, stoned and thinly sliced
- handful lovage leaves
- 2 handfuls mixed baby salad leaves
- sherry vinegar, to taste
- salt, to taste
- black pepper, to taste

Brush the courgettes with olive oil and grill in a very hot griddle pan until just cooked.

Toss with the sliced nectarines, lovage and baby leaves. Season with a splash of sherry vinegar, and some salt and black pepper. Add a slick of olive oil if you like.

SORGHUM, CORN, CHARD

AND HERB SALAD | SERVES 10

THE MUSTARD VINAIGRETTE
- 2 tablespoons wholegrain mustard
- ½ clove garlic, finely chopped
- 2 tablespoons sherry vinegar
- 2 tablespoons finely diced red onion
- salt, to taste
- 5 tablespoons olive oil

Mix the mustard, garlic, vinegar and onion together and season with salt.

Slowly whisk in the oil, until well incorporated. Set aside until needed.

THE SORGHUM SALAD
- 300 g cooked sorghum grains
- corn kernels from 1 husk, raw
- ½ red onion, finely diced
- 300 g chard, finely sliced
- handful each of basil leaves, dill and parsley, all roughly chopped

Mix all the ingredients together and season with mustard vinaigrette, salt and black pepper.

Instead of sorghum, you could also try quinoa or another similar grain.

CHOCOLATE PAVLOVA

WITH PASSION FRUIT SABAYON AND FRESH BERRIES | SERVES 10

CHOCOLATE MERINGUE

- 2 tablespoons cocoa powder
- 2 tablespoons boiling water
- 175 g egg whites (left over from the sabayon)
- 225 g castor sugar
- 2 teaspoons cornflour
- 1 teaspoon white wine vinegar

Preheat the oven to 120 °C. Mix the cocoa powder and water together well.

Whisk the egg whites until stiff peaks form. Slowly add the sugar while whisking until all the sugar has dissolved and the meringue has stiff peaks. Transfer to a big bowl and fold in the cornflour and white wine vinegar.

Fold in the cocoa mix and then spoon onto a tray, lined with silicone paper. Remember that this will be the base of the dessert so make sure it is nice and deep, with high edges. Bake for 1 hour, cool and set aside until you are ready to serve.

PASSION FRUIT SABAYON

- 1 cup passion fruit pulp
- 7 high-quality, free-range egg yolks
- 100 g castor sugar
- pinch of salt
- 250 ml cream, whipped
- 2 cups mixed fresh berries

Place the passion fruit in a small pot and reduce to 150 ml. Strain out the pips.

Mix the egg yolks with the sugar, salt and passion fruit in a stainless steel bowl. Place the bowl over a pot with 3 cm of simmering water. (The bowl must not touch the water.)

Whisk continuously until the eggs are cooked and very fluffy. Take off the heat and leave to cool. Fold through the whipped cream.

To assemble the pavlova, pipe the sabayon onto the meringue and add fresh berries to garnish.

MARTHINUS FERREIRA

Zarzuela and Mom's famous garlic bread
Smoked ham hock and foie gras terrine
Couscous salad
Cherry bakewell tart

You could say Marthinus Ferreira came from nowhere. You'd be wrong. With stints in some highly respected kitchens (including a time with Heston Blumenthal at The Fat Duck), the guy has skills. He was always going to be a major success somewhere. So why didn't we hear about him sooner? Well one or two bad breaks left him out in the cold a few years ago. At a bit of a crossroads, he made the ballsy decision to start up his own place. He hasn't looked back.

dw eleven-13 is one of the most celebrated restaurants in the country, let alone Joburg. Marthinus is banging out food to fully-booked dinner and lunch services and has expanded by opening Grazing Room, the adjacent tapas bar. His food is uncomplicated and his philosophy is that the main ingredients on the plate should be celebrated, not disguised with sauces. Marthinus chooses to focus on flavour. And he nails it every time. The fact that his restaurant manages to do so well, while being hidden around the back of a building and boasting a parking lot as a view, should tell you something about the quality of the food and the commitment of the chef.

The place is a family affair, with his mom, his dad and his sister all lending a hand in helping steer the ship – which makes it even cooler that they are all there when we arrive for a Sunday lunch.

Marthinus has been whetting my appetite for a few days prior, with hints of what he's cooking. When I arrive I'm not disappointed. Mountains of fresh mussels, langoustines, crayfish and prawns are piled up around the kitchen. He picks up one of the crayfish and throws it to me. "Not bad hey? My mate got these to me from Hermanus especially for today." Marthinus is committed to sourcing local and seasonal ingredients wherever possible, so the gesture is not lost on me. Everything goes into a zarzuela (a Spanish fish stew), along with some saffron, white wine, garlic and chilli. Marthinus makes it all look ridiculously easy – but I don't know how he manages to get any cooking done in between all the talking, waving of arms and pouring of wine!

And that wine. Dear me. It deserves a mention. White Rioja, French Pinot, French Rosé. It's phenomenal stuff. The important thing is the way it's served though, with none of the stuffiness you'd expect. This ability to make high-end food and drink accessible is the hallmark of his restaurant.

Next up: a ham hock and foie gras terrine that people must "nibble while they wait". Awesome. A simple salad accompanies it, with some of his aunt's preserved figs mixed through the micro greens. He knocks up a few sides, referring to the garlic bread and the couscous salad as "undoubtedly my Mom's recipes".

South Africa is playing cricket at The Wanderers (a game for which Marthinus had tickets) and I apologise for ruining his day. He brushes me off on the way to the TV to turn the game on. With a massive smile, an even bigger glass of wine and a gesture towards the screen he asks me, "Where would you rather be?" I must say, he has a point.

ZARZUELA

SERVES 8

- 4 red peppers, very finely sliced
- 2 white onions, very finely sliced
- 2 fennel bulbs, very finely sliced
- 2 large red chillies, deseeded and finely chopped
- 2 cloves garlic, crushed
- 100 ml olive oil
- 100 g butter (plus 100 g extra)
- 2 g Spanish saffron
- 100 g ground almonds
- 16 medium langoustine tails
- 8 crayfish tails, cut in half lengthways
- 1 kg deveined queen prawns, shell on
- 400 ml good white wine
- 2 kg fresh mussels, scrubbed and de-bearded
- 850 ml tinned Italian tomatoes, blended until smooth
- salt and pepper
- 2 whole lemons, cut in half
- 150 g finely chopped parsley

Preheat your oven to 160 °C. In the biggest cast iron pot you have, fry off the peppers, onions, fennel, chilli and garlic with the olive oil and 100 g of the butter until soft. Stir the saffron and ground almonds into the mixture.

Add the langoustines, crayfish tails and prawns, and cook for a few seconds, or until they take on a bit of colour. Deglaze with the white wine, then add the mussels and tinned tomatoes before covering the pot. Cook in the oven for 1 hour.

Remove from the oven and season with salt and pepper. Squeeze the lemons into the sauce, using a sieve to catch any seeds.

Drop the lemons into the pot and finish with the fresh parsley and the extra butter.

MOM'S FAMOUS GARLIC BREAD

SERVES 8

- 4 bulbs garlic
- olive oil
- coarse salt
- 150 g unsalted butter
- ½ cup finely chopped parsley
- 1 tub cream cheese
- 3 baguettes

Preheat the oven to 150 °C. Place the garlic bulbs in an oven-proof dish, drizzle with olive oil and coarse salt and bake for about an hour, or until soft. Allow to cool.

Meanwhile, mix the butter, parsley and cream cheese together at room temperature. When cool, squeeze the garlic from their skins and combine with the butter mixture.

Cut the baguettes into thick slices and spread generously with the garlic mixture. Cover with tin foil and bake in the oven (still at 150 °C) for about 8 minutes, or until crispy.

Use to mop up the incredible broth left behind from the zarzuela.

SMOKED HAM HOCK

AND FOIE GRAS TERRINE | SERVES 8

- 10 thin slices Parma ham
- 1 onion, finely chopped
- 1 carrot, finely chopped
- 3 – 4 thyme sprigs
- 6 whole black peppercorns
- 250 ml dry white wine
- 4 smoked ham hocks
- 1 cup chopped flat leaf parsley
- 100 g wholegrain mustard
- 150 g foie gras
- 2 preserved figs, quartered
- 2 spring onions, thinly sliced
- rocket leaves (micro leaves, if possible)

Lightly grease a one-litre terrine tray. Line with plastic wrap, leaving a generous overhang. Layer the Parma ham over the plastic.

Place the onion, carrot, thyme, peppercorns and wine in a large saucepan. Cover with cold water and bring to the boil, skimming off any impurities that rise to the surface. Reduce heat to low, add your ham hocks and simmer for 3 hours or until the ham is very tender. Remove from the heat and allow the ham to cool in the pan.

Remove the ham and discard the solids and most of the cooking liquid, reserving 250 ml. Skin the hocks and flake the meat from the bone – you should have about 1 kg of meat. Combine with the parsley and wholegrain mustard.

Strain the reserved liquid into a small pan and warm over a low heat. Pack some of the flaked meat tightly into the terrine, add the foie gras to the middle of the terrine, then finish packing the rest of the pork meat on top of that. Carefully pour over the cooking liquid so that it completely covers your layered terrine (you may not need it all). Allow to cool, then fold in the overhanging plastic wrap using the Parma ham to create the top layer.

Chill for 2 hours, then place some thick cardboard over the terrine and place weights or cans on top. This will allow the terrine to set overnight.

To serve, slice to desired thickness and garnish with figs, spring onions and salad leaves.

COUSCOUS SALAD

SERVES 8

- 500 g couscous
- 1 cube stock (chicken or vegetable)
- 250 ml boiling water
- 60 ml olive oil
- 1 punnet mange tout peas, roughly chopped and sautéed
- 1 punnet baby corn, roughly chopped and sautéed
- 1 punnet asparagus, roughly chopped and sautéed
- 1 packet spring onions, finely sliced
- 1 red pepper, deseeded, finely sliced and sautéed
- 3 cloves garlic, crushed and sautéed
- 1 cup chopped parsley
- salt and pepper, to taste
- 1 cup chopped coriander
- 50 g roasted pine nuts

Empty the couscous into a large bowl and dissolve the stock cube in a cup of boiling water. Add the stock and the olive oil to the couscous. Pour in some more boiling water, so that the couscous is only just covered, and cover the bowl with cling wrap.

Allow to stand for 10 minutes, remove the cling wrap and use a fork to fluff up the grains.

Stir in your vegetables, garlic and parsley. Season to taste and garnish with chopped coriander and pine nuts. Drizzle with some extra olive oil if necessary.

CHERRY BAKEWELL TART

SERVES 8 – 10

THE PASTRY

- 300 g plain flour, plus extra for dusting
- 125 g unsalted butter
- 30 g sugar
- 1 free-range egg (plus 1 extra, beaten, to glaze)
- 2 tablespoons milk, to bind (if needed)

Preheat the oven to 200 °C. Place the flour, butter, sugar and egg in a food processor and pulse to combine. If necessary, add a little milk to help bring the mixture together.

Turn the dough out onto a floured work surface and roll out until large enough to line a 26 cm tin. Carefully lift the pastry into the tin, then place it in the fridge to chill for an hour.

Line the pastry with a sheet of greaseproof paper, weighed down with baking beans or rice. Bake blind in the oven for 15 to 20 minutes. Remove the paper and beans and brush the pastry all over with the beaten egg.

Return the pastry shell to the oven for a further 5 minutes, until golden-brown. Remove from the oven and turn the temperature down to 180 °C.

THE FILLING

- 225 g butter, softened
- 225 g sugar
- 225 g ground almonds
- 3 free-range eggs
- finely grated zest of 1 lemon
- 50 g plain flour
- 1 jar good-quality cherry jam
- 200 g fresh cherries, stoned
- flaked almonds, for garnish

Beat the butter and sugar together in a bowl until pale and fluffy. Mix in the ground almonds, then crack in the eggs one at a time, beating well between each addition – don't worry if the mixture begins to separate, just add a little of the flour. Fold in the lemon zest and the flour.

Spread some of the jam generously across the base of the pastry case, leaving a 2.5 mm gap around the edge. Cover with the fresh cherries. Pour and spread the filling mixture over the jam and cherries, so that everything is nicely covered.

Bake for 20 minutes, or until set and golden-brown. Allow to cool in the tin before serving in slices.

Garnish with flaked almonds and serve with ice cream or whipped cream.

MASSIMO & TRACY ORIONE

Few things spark a food debate amongst friends and family as quickly as the question, "Where can I get the best pizza?" We all think we have a secret little spot that makes the best version of this humble dish. A few years ago I met a guy who settled that question for me once and for all. Since discovering Massimo's in Hout Bay, I return whenever I can and I preach to anybody who will listen that his pizza is the best in the land. So far, I haven't had anyone disagree.

But Massimo is about more than pizza. I mention it merely to illustrate his philosophy towards food as a whole: get the best raw ingredients you can and do as little to them as possible. His dough is made from stone-ground flour, his tomato sauce is a guarded secret and his toppings are seasonal, premium products that are used sparingly. He's a true artisan and, together with his wife Tracy, he makes some of the tastiest food in Cape Town. It's a solid team, with Tracy providing most of the ideas and Massimo executing them. The result might not be the prettiest food around, but it's the type that makes me smile.

What kind of people are Massimo and Tracy? Well, after meeting them years ago I have since become a regular at their restaurant, have had business meetings at their home and we have worked on several projects together. Even so, when I began this chapter it was the first time I realized I didn't know their surname! (It's Orione by the way.) To be able to build a working relationship, as well as a friendship, knowing only their first names proves what kind of people they are. Casual, generous, inviting, honest and always happiest with a full glass of wine or a cold beer.

The shoot is exactly as I'd hoped. A long table, set in their restaurant on the day they are closed, is what they've convinced me is the best way to have a relaxed, mid-week lunch. "How can I cook for you without my wood-burning oven?" was Massimo's (incredibly serious) question. The man had a point. And so began an authentic, Italian lunch.

On the day, with rain being whipped against rattling windows, Massimo's point was further vindicated. With the oven providing warmth – and the beer and wine amplifying it – dishes are passed around the table like an Italian conveyor belt. Focaccia, aubergines, anchovies, fresh salsa verde, goat's cheese, fennel salad, a flurry of pizzas, roasted garlic and vegetables, chocolate and rum dessert. And more. (Later, when we got round to editing the recipes, it would transpire that we had no less than 11 to choose from!) And the common theme? Less is more. Well, in terms of ingredients. Certainly not in terms of quantity.

All good things do eventually come to an end though, and this epic lunch winds down verrrrrry slowly. Some blame the weather, but I don't buy it. It could be a belter outside and they would want their guests to stay for a bit more. They're those kind of people. It's that kind of food.

FENNEL SALAD

SERVES 4 – 6

- 2 fennel bulbs, outer layers and stems removed
- 1 cup crushed walnuts
- salt and pepper, to taste
- olive oil, to taste (the best you can find)
- 1 cup shaved Parmesan (the best you can find)

Finely slice the fresh fennel (use a mandolin slicer if possible, otherwise use a very sharp knife). Toss the fennel with the crushed walnuts and salt and pepper. Add a good glug of olive oil and mix with your hands to ensure everything is well coated. Finish with the shaved Parmesan and serve.

TIP: Only use big fat bulbs, not the "baby fennel" which is too often dry.

MASSIMO'S MAMMA'S GIARDINIERA

PICKLED VEGETABLE SALSA | MAKES SEVERAL JARS

- 300 g celery
- 300 g onion
- 300 g carrot
- 300 g green beans
- 300 g peppers
- 4 cans good-quality tinned tomatoes
- 250 ml extra virgin olive oil
- 500 ml red wine vinegar
- 2 tablespoons sugar
- 1 tablespoon salt
- 1 nutmeg, freshly grated

Cut all the vegetables into small pieces, roughly the same size. Combine all the ingredients in a medium-sized pot. Bring to a gentle boil and cook for exactly 40 minutes.

Cool and fill sterilised glass jars (it will make several, but they last for months). Making sure that the jars are properly closed, place them in a deep pot and cover with cold water. Bring to a boil and simmer for 20 minutes. Remove the jars from the pot and allow them to cool.

Use the giardiniera as required – brilliant with cold meats or good cheese.

SALSA VERDE

"GREEN SAUCE" | SERVES 4 – 6

- 1 large bunch Italian flat leaf parsley
- 2 anchovies
- 1 boiled egg, yolk only
- 1 clove garlic
- extra virgin olive oil

In a blender, mix the parsley leaves, anchovies, egg yolk, garlic and enough olive oil to create a thick, luxurious sauce. Ideal with fresh goat's cheese as part of an antipasto platter.

AUBERGINE SALAD

SERVES 4 – 6

- 2 aubergines, sliced very thinly lengthways
- olive oil, for brushing
- salt and pepper
- 100 ml olive oil
- 2 tablespoons cider vinegar
- 2 cloves garlic, crushed and sautéed
- 1 handful fresh basil leaves, left whole

Brush the aubergines with olive oil and season with salt and pepper. Cook on the braai or in a griddle pan until nicely charred.

Make a marinade of the olive oil, cider vinegar, garlic and fresh basil. Pour over the aubergines while still warm, and leave for as long as possible (even overnight is fine). Serve as part of an antipasto platter.

BAGNA CAUDA

"WARM SAUCE" | SERVES 6

- 2 heads of garlic
- milk, to cover
- 2 jars anchovies
- 50 g butter
- 50 ml extra virgin olive oil
- fresh cream

Peel the garlic heads and cut each clove into 2 or 3 pieces. Place the garlic in a small saucepan and cover the chopped cloves with milk, cooking slowly until soft (add more milk if necessary).

Add the anchovies, butter and olive oil. Cook on low heat for 10 minutes until the anchovies are completely melted. Add a few tablespoons of fresh cream just before serving.

Serve in a heat-proof pot with a warming candle, or simply spoon the sauce over your warm vegetables. Traditional options include raw cabbage leaves, roasted peppers, boiled potatoes or roasted onions, but use whatever vegetables you enjoy. It is also very good as a pasta sauce.

PIZZA MELANZANE PARMIGIANA
Tomato base, roasted slices of aubergine, topped with more tomato sauce, *fior di latte* mozzarella and Parmesan. Before serving, add basil oil and fresh basil leaves.

PIZZA MONTAGNA
White base brushed with melted garlic and herb butter, good cheese, braised red cabbage and Black Forest ham.

PIZZA AGLIO
Tomato base, soft goat's cheese, whole garlic cloves previously roasted with olive oil, and fresh thyme.

THE BEST PIZZAS IN TOWN

MAKES ENOUGH FOR 8 SMALL OR 6 LARGE ONES

BASIC PIZZA DOUGH
- 20 g fresh yeast
- 500 ml warm tap water
- 1 kg plain flour
- 1 tablespoon fine salt
- 2 tablespoons olive oil, if making pizza in a regular oven

Dissolve the yeast in warm water for 10 minutes. Mix the dry ingredients together, making a well in the centre. Pour in the dissolved yeast, add extra water, and oil if using, and slowly (bit by bit) bring together with one hand, keeping the other dry. (The quantity of water you use depends on humidity levels, so you may need to add a little more.)

Keep at it until the mixture comes away from the sides of the bowl. You cannot do this with a spoon, but it can be done using a food mixer with a dough hook. The end result you're after is for the dough to be slightly wet and soft.

Your dry hand will come in useful to remove the dough stuck to your other hand. Have some flour nearby to help with this.

Place the dough in a bowl large enough for it to double in size, and cover with a damp tea towel or cling film. Leave in a warm, draught-free place for as long as you can (overnight is best, but for at least 3 hours). The dough should have doubled in size by then.

Flour your work surface and your rolling pin well, take a suitably-sized piece of dough and get rolling. Keep turning the dough as it will easily stick to the rolling pin.

If you want to make a perfect round each time, pick the dough up and give it a half turn before you continue rolling. Only practice makes perfect.

Alternatively, you can also fill a rectangular baking tray. Don't roll the dough too thick as it may not cook through. Rub a little oil on your baking tray to prevent sticking and, if using a domestic oven, make sure it has been on its highest setting for at least 10 minutes before cooking.

Top with your favourite ingredients and bake the pizzas for 8 to 10 minutes, depending on your oven.

SGROPPINO

MAKES 6 SMALL GLASSES

- 3 scoops lemon ice cream
- 1 shot vodka
- 2 shots Methode Cap Classique
- 2 shots free-range milk

In a blender mix the lemon ice cream, vodka, Cap Classique and milk. Adjust quantities if necessary until it is creamy. Serve in champagne glasses, as a palate cleanser between courses.

BUNET

"LITTLE HAT" OR "BONNET" | SERVES 6

- 4 free-range egg yolks
- 2 whole free-range eggs
- 80 g cocoa
- 200 g castor sugar
- 100 g amaretti biscuits, finely crushed
- 1 litre free-range milk, at room temperature
- 250 ml rum

Preheat your oven to 180 °C. Beat the egg yolks, the whole eggs and the cocoa together with half the sugar until smooth. Add the amaretti and the tepid milk, along with the rum. Stir, making sure that there are no lumps at all.

Caramelise the rest of the sugar and pour some into prepared moulds. Work quickly so that the sugar doesn't set before you pour an equal amount of the cocoa mixture into each mould.

Bake in the oven in a *bain-marie* for approximately 1 hour, or until a skewer comes out clean. Carefully place the moulds in cold water, so that only the bottom of the mould is covered. Allow to cool completely before turning out onto a plate.

Serve, garnished with some extra crushed amaretti biscuits sprinkled over the plate.

MICHAEL BROUGHTON

Sugar-cured loin of tuna with baby salad leaves and avocado
Oven-roasted shoulder of lamb with its own jus
Crispy potatoes & Roasted vegetables
Milk chocolate and hazelnut bar
Macaroons

Never trust a skinny chef. Right? Wrong. Meet Michael Broughton, the man behind the perennially successful Terroir at Kleine Zalze Estate, outside Stellenbosch. Unofficially known as The King of Sauces, the guy is a genius at taking classical French techniques and adding little kicks from all over the globe. He can serve a plate of food with a clear and well thought-out idea of how the sauce can accentuate it. Complete it. Add an extra dimension to it. Lift it without overpowering it. It's this philosophy – along with the insistence on using only the finest local, seasonal produce – that has earned him a loyal following. With trends and fads coming and going, Michael's attention to detail is what keeps people coming back for more.

The same respect for food shines through in his kitchen at home. We've asked Michael to keep things simple, and his menu is bang on, but the inner-perfectionist is hard at work. I watch him going through the motions. Measurements are exact. Knife work is flawless. Portion sizes are identical. Plates are beautifully presented.

Sure, he's relaxed, but his food looks like it's been plucked from the pages of a magazine. I joke with his lovely wife Jane that he couldn't be messy if he tried. It's confirmed with a knowing nod, as we both watch impeccable plates of food being assembled.

I'd been eyeing some chicken roasting on the Weber but it turns out that was just for the kids! Instead, simply-cured tuna kicks off the meal on a light note before being followed by beautifully cooked lamb, crispy golden potatoes and one of those famous sauces, in the form of a rich jus.

A chocolate and hazelnut mousse is dished up to the masses too. And I do mean masses; there are, on my count, at least 8 kids and as many parents.

A few hours into the day and it's all about those kids. Some are in the pool. Some are in their rooms blaring Lemonade Mouth. Tennis balls collide with rugby balls, and at one stage (I'm not making this up) a foam dart ends up in the dessert. For anyone else it would be a zoo, but Michael is as composed as ever, hardly breaking a sweat. In fact, scrap that. He doesn't even come close to breaking a sweat. Instead kids are invited into the kitchen to help prep the macaroons, which are served as a pièce de résistance. His are infused with beetroot and laced with a carrot butter cream. Served with fresh coffee, they're an unusual and utterly cool way to end the meal.

With the car acting as a metal cocoon away from kids, dogs and tween bands, the drive back to Cape Town is relatively quiet. He might be skinny, but put him a kitchen and I'd trust Michael Broughton any day.

SUGAR-CURED LOIN OF TUNA

WITH BABY SALAD LEAVES AND AVOCADO | SERVES 4

THE LOIN OF TUNA

- 100 g sugar
- 200 g coarse salt
- 1 tablespoon roasted and ground coriander
- 1 tablespoon roasted and ground Szechuan peppercorns (or ½ tablespoon white pepper)
- 1 tot brandy
- 500 g cleaned eye of tuna (skinned, deboned and with no blood line)

Mix all ingredients (except the tuna) in a bowl. Line your work surface with cling film, so that it overlaps. Sprinkle the area nearest to you with a layer of the sugar mixture, and place the fish down on top of it, making sure the entire loin will be covered with the sugary spices. Wrap cling film tightly around the tuna, and place in the fridge for 1½ hours and allow to cure.

Remove the plastic, wash the cure off the fish, pat dry and re-roll tightly with clean cling film. Cut into very thin slices with an extremely sharp knife. Remove the plastic from each slice of fish and plate.

THE SAUCE

- 3 tablespoons mirin
- 4 teaspoons rice wine vinegar
- 1 tablespoon light soy sauce
- 1 teaspoon lime juice
- pinch of sugar
- pinch of salt
- ¼ red onion, very finely diced
- 3 cm ginger, peeled and very finely diced

Stir everything together and chill for a few hours to allow the flavours to infuse.

Spoon over the tuna slices just before serving.

THE VINAIGRETTE

- 1 tablespoon white wine vinegar
- 1 tablespoon sherry vinegar
- 1 tablespoon lemon juice
- ½ teaspoon mustard
- 50 ml olive oil
- 50 ml extra virgin olive oil
- salt and pepper

Whisk the acids and mustard together well. While still whisking, slowly add the oils until emulsified. Season, cover and chill till needed.

Toss through the baby salad leaves just before serving.

THE AVOCADO SALAD

- 1 large, ripe avocado
- juice of 1 lemon
- 2 tablespoons extra virgin olive oil
- salt and pepper (be generous)
- baby salad leaves

Peel and cut the avocado into 2 cm cubes. Squeeze over the lemon juice and add the oil. Season well and gently fold together so that everything is combined.

To serve, place a few slices of tuna on a plate in a straight line. Toss some baby salad leaves through your vinaigrette. Place leaves along the side of your tuna, and spoon over some of the sauce. Finish off by placing a few avocado cubes on or around the fish.

OVEN-ROASTED SHOULDER OF LAMB

WITH ITS OWN JUS | SERVES 8

BASIL CRUST

- 2 large handfuls basil leaves
- 1 loaf white bread, crusts removed and dried out in the oven for 2 hours
- 2 cloves garlic, peeled and sliced
- salt and pepper

Make this in advance and use whenever you need it. Fry the basil leaves in oil at 140°C for 30 seconds or until the leaves are shiny. Do this in batches and be very careful as the oil does "spit" – it could burn you.

Remove the leaves with a slotted spoon and place onto paper towels to drain. Break the bread into pieces and blend together with the garlic in a food processor until smooth. Add the basil leaves, and salt and pepper to taste. Blitz again briefly and keep in an airtight container.

LAMB JUS

- bone from the shoulder
- 500 g extra lamb bones (ask your butcher to cube them into chunks; loin or neck bones work well)
- 3 tablespoons olive oil
- 2 large carrots
- 2 onions, roughly diced
- 1 head garlic, cut in half
- 2 large stalks celery, leaves removed
- 225 ml dry white wine
- 30 g tomato paste
- 1 litre chicken stock
- 1 bay leaf
- 1 small bunch thyme
- 4 sprigs rosemary
- 1 teaspoon lemon juice

Make the sauce while the lamb is roasting. Brown the bones in a hot pot with the olive oil. Roast them in the oven at 190°C until browned. Drain off the oil and set aside.

In the same pot, add the carrots and continue to brown over medium heat. Add the onions and brown them too. Add the garlic, pushing it flat on the base of the pot.

Don't move the veggies for 6 minutes, until they have some decent colour on them.

Add the celery and the bones and allow everything to begin to fry again. Add the wine and cook it dry. Add the tomato paste and cook for 5 to 8 minutes before adding the stock, the bay leaf, the thyme and half of the rosemary.

If the bones are sticking, add a little more stock. Bring to a gentle simmer and skim off the froth and fat that comes to the surface. Simmer for an hour.

Strain the sauce through a fine sieve, add the rest of the rosemary and reduce to about half its volume. If necessary you can thicken it with a little cornflour.

Check the seasoning and add the lemon juice to sharpen it a little. Cover and keep warm.

SHOULDER OF LAMB

- **3.2 kg shoulder of lamb, deboned (ask your butcher to do this)**
- **2 tablespoons finely chopped garlic**
- **salt and pepper**
- **olive oil**
- **2 teaspoons thyme leaves**
- **125 ml red wine**
- **prepared mustard**
- **basil crust**

Lay the lamb shoulder out on a work surface and remove about a third of the visible fat. Rub over half the garlic, season with salt and pepper and re-role into its original shape. Secure the roll with string, making sure it's not too tight.

Heat some oil until smoking and sear your meat until nicely coloured on all sides (a few minutes should do it). Transfer the roll to a roasting pan and allow the meat to cool.

Rub with the remaining garlic and the thyme, and season well once more. Add a splash of wine to the pan, cover tightly with tinfoil and roast in a preheated oven at 160 °C for 3 to 3 ½ hours, or until deliciously sticky and soft.

Remove the string and set meat aside to rest. (Make your sauce while the lamb is roasting.)

Just before serving, smear the lamb with mustard, dust your work surface with some basil crust and roll the lamb in the mixture to make sure it is evenly coated with a good crust. It doesn't matter if the lamb breaks up a bit.

Carve and serve with the jus, roast potatoes and vegetables (see recipes on page 174).

CRISPY ROAST POTATOES

- 8 medium potatoes
- 350 ml sunflower oil
- 2 teaspoons finely chopped rosemary
- 1 teaspoon finely chopped garlic
- sea salt
- freshly ground black pepper

TIP: Don't use Mediterranean or any other waxy potatoes. Rather get the dry fluffy ones.

Preheat your oven to 180°C. Place the potatoes in a pot of cold water and bring to the simmer. Don't boil them fast, as they will split and absorb water. When the tip of a small knife goes through with little resistance, they are done. (This should take about 30 minutes.)

Place your roasting tin on the stove, with the oil in it. Heat the tin over one or two stove plates. Meanwhile drain the potatoes and let them cool only slightly, then peel off the skins. Cut the potatoes into any shape (don't worry if they crumble slightly – they'll just end up more crispy) and quickly and carefully put the potatoes into the hot oil.

Bake in the oven until lightly golden on the undersides and then turn them over and roast the other side. Five minutes from the end, throw over the chopped rosemary and garlic and stir the potatoes.

Remove from the oven, sprinkle generously with salt and pepper, then drain on a few layers of paper towel.

Whatever you do, do not cover them as they will steam and lose their crunch. Rather turn off the oven and keep them warm in there. Serve with the oven-roasted lamb (page 170).

ROASTED VEGETABLES

- 2 medium aubergines
- ½ cup olive oil
- salt and pepper
- 4 cloves garlic, peeled and sliced
- 4 medium tomatoes
- 2 large courgettes
- 1 teaspoon thyme leaves
- a few extra sprigs of thyme

Preheat the oven to 180°C. Slice the aubergines into about ½ cm slices and fry in half the oil until lightly browned. Season with salt and pepper, and drain on kitchen paper.

Blitz the rest of the olive oil with the garlic until smooth. Slice the tomatoes ½ cm thick, and the courgettes slightly thinner. Season everything with salt and pepper, thyme and the garlic oil mixture.

Grease a small roasting tray and layer the vegetables, alternating them with one another. The trick is to stand them upright, using them to support each other. Sprinkle again with salt and pepper, add the extra sprigs of thyme and bake for 15 minutes. If they are not cooked through, leave them in for a little longer.

Serve with the oven-roasted lamb (page 170).

MILK CHOCOLATE
AND HAZELNUT BAR | SERVES 8

THE BASE
- 75 g hazelnuts, roasted, skinned and roughly chopped
- 75 g castor sugar
- 2 egg whites
- 30 g icing sugar, sieved

Preheat the oven to 170 °C. Grease a 30 cm x 20 cm baking sheet, and set aside.

Blitz the nuts and castor sugar together until finely ground. Beat the egg whites to form medium peaks, slowly add the icing sugar and continue to beat until stiff peaks form.

Fold in the hazelnut and sugar mixture, and spread on the baking sheet, so that the layer is about 3 to 4 mm thick.

Bake for 8 minutes, or until slightly crisp. Remove and allow to cool.

MILK CHOCOLATE MOUSSE
- 400 g milk chocolate (the very best you can get)
- 225 g 70% dark chocolate (the very best you can get)
- 500 ml cream, whipped to resemble the texture of yoghurt

Melt the chocolate over a pot of simmering water, mix together well and allow to cool.

Very gently fold the chocolate mixture into the cream and pour onto the hazelnut base to about 3 cm high. Smooth off and chill for 2 hours.

THE CHOCOLATE GLAZE
- 150 ml water
- 175 g castor sugar
- 55 g cocoa
- 125 ml cream
- 40 g 70% dark chocolate
- 2 ½ gelatine leaves, soaked in some cold water

Add all the ingredients (except the gelatine) to a saucepan and bring to the boil. Simmer for 5 to 6 minutes, remove from the heat and whisk in the softened gelatine leaves.

Allow the chocolate to cool and pour the glaze over the cold mousse, tilting the tray as you go to achieve a smooth and shiny finish. Don't be tempted to try to flatten the glaze; you will make it cloudy if you fiddle with it. (If you really want to, you can run a kitchen blowtorch over it before serving it to get the shiny effect.)

To serve, warm a knife and carefully cut into 3 cm x 8 cm slices. Serve with some caramel ice cream and garnish with ground toasted hazelnuts.

BASIC MACAROON RECIPE

MAKES ABOUT 20 MACAROONS

- 250 g ground almonds
- 250 g icing sugar
- 200 g egg whites
- 200 g castor sugar

Preheat the oven to 100 °C. Sieve the almonds and icing sugar. Beat the egg whites until soft peaks form and slowly add the castor sugar, continuing to beat until you're left with a stiff meringue mixture.

Fold in the sieved ingredients and gently fold to combine. Using a piping bag, pipe into small circles and allow them to sit uncovered for 20 minutes to form a skin. Bake for 15 to 20 minutes.

When ready, make a butter cream and sandwich it between two macaroon sides. Serve with coffee.

NOTE: You can add a wide variety of flavours to macaroons. These are beetroot with a carrot butter cream, so let your creativity come through when experimenting!

PETE GOFFE-WOOD

Sauté of squid with chorizo and butter beans
Mexican spice-rubbed tuna loin tortillas

H out Bay. Well … the Republic of Hout Bay to be exact. How fancy. Quite what that means I'm not sure – nobody has ever been able to explain it to me. Anyway, that's neither here nor there. It's a gorgeous day and that's where we're headed.

We're meeting up with Pete Goffe-Wood and his wife Elize. Having spent years in various top kitchens throughout the country, Pete's main focus nowadays is on teaching men how to cook through his (awesomely-named) cookery school, Kitchen Cowboys. Elize is a mean cook too, and together they run The Kitchen Cowboys Canteen from Woodstock, where top-quality ingredients are cooked up simply, often with Indian flavours. Generally known as the Master of Seafood, Pete is heavily involved with SASSI (South African Sustainable Seafood Initiative) and I'm hoping to see some fresh seafood on his lunch menu.

Naturally we stop at the harbour on our way. There's something very cool about the Hout Bay harbour. Fishermen unload their catch, scattering seagulls everywhere as their wet nets slap the dock. Long bandages of white sand stretch out towards restaurants, where people are happily enjoying the sunshine and some cold wine. We stumble across a local fisherman who seems to have had a particularly festive morning. (It's about 10 am.) He balances an almost-empty bottle of wine on his crooked elbow and tries to sell me the cactus that he's cradling in the other

arm. "No thanks, I'm cool," I reply, thinking this should be the end of it. But our guy is pretty determined. "How about some boxing or Muay Thai lessons then?" he offers, to my surprise. I've got to be honest, I didn't see that one coming. You've got to love the entrepreneurial spirit of the Hout Bay locals.

We're still laughing at the whole thing, when we arrive at the Goffe-Woods. Pete greets us barefoot, and within 5 minutes a cold beer has found its way into my hand. It's now about 11 am. A Weber is wheeled outside, and the coals are lit. Guests arrive, each seemingly determined to bring a better bottle of wine than the next one. Pete opens them with the insightful explanation, "If not now, then when?" (A mantra that I swear to take away with me.)

My seafood prayers are answered, and what follows is a meal fresh from the ocean. Calamari is sautéed with chorizo and butter beans, with the main attraction being one of the most beautiful hunks of tuna I've ever seen. Sticking with the casual approach, Pete rubs it with cumin and chilli and cooks it on the grid. He then slices it and presents it with various sides as part of a top-notch Mexican feast.

A monumental cheese board is presented as dessert. It's laid out for people to help themselves, but everybody needs a breather first. In this house, at this lunch, a breather means another glass of that special but-let's-drink-it-anyway wine. They've got it right out there in The Republic.

181

SAUTÉ OF SQUID

WITH CHORIZO AND BUTTER BEANS | SERVES 4

- vegetable oil
- 100 g chorizo, sliced
- 200 g squid
- 3 tomatoes, blanched, peeled and roughly chopped
- 1 tin butter beans, drained
- 2 cloves garlic, finely chopped
- 1 cup flat leaf parsley, roughly chopped (reserve a pinch for garnish)
- 100 g unsalted butter
- juice of 1 lemon
- sea salt
- freshly ground black pepper

Heat a little oil in a hot sauté pan. Add the chorizo. When it begins to take on some colour add the squid followed by the roughly chopped tomatoes.

As the tomatoes begin to break down, add the butter beans, garlic, chopped parsley, butter and the lemon juice. Adjust the seasoning with salt and ground black pepper.

When the butter has melted, remove the pan from the heat and serve immediately.

MEXICAN SPICE-RUBBED
TUNA LOIN TORTILLAS | SERVES 6

THE MEXICAN SPICE RUB

- 1 teaspoon crushed red chillies
- 1 tablespoon whole coriander seeds
- 1 tablespoon whole cumin seeds
- 1 teaspoon smoked paprika
- 50 ml extra virgin olive oil
- juice of 2 limes
- salt and pepper

Dry-fry the spices in a pan until roasted. Grind all the spices with a pestle and mortar until well blended.

Combine with the oil and lime juice to make a paste, and season with salt and pepper. Set aside.

This spice rub is a cracker and can be used on chicken and meat too.

THE TUNA

- 1 kg tuna loin

Rub the spice paste all over the tuna and leave to marinade for 20 minutes.

Place the tuna on an oiled braai grid and cook it for 2 to 4 minutes on each side, making sure you keep it nice and rare. (The tuna can be done in a hot griddle pan too.) Allow to rest for a few minutes and cut into thin slices.

Set aside until you are ready to assemble the tortillas.

THE TOMATO SALSA

- 1 red onion
- 1 chilli
- 1 clove garlic
- thumb-sized piece of ginger
- juice of 2 limes (or lemons)
- 6 tomatoes, roughly chopped
- fresh coriander
- 100 ml olive oil
- 1 teaspoon sugar
- salt and pepper

Finely chop the onion, chilli, garlic and ginger, and combine with the lime juice. Leave to infuse while chopping the tomatoes.

Roughly tear the coriander and add the tomato and the coriander to the onion mix. Add the olive oil and sugar, mix well and adjust the seasoning, adding salt and pepper to taste. Set aside, allowing the flavours to develop.

THE GUACAMOLE

- **2 ripe avocados**
- **1 red chilli**
- **thumb-sized piece of ginger, grated**
- **½ cup Greek yoghurt**
- **½ cup roughly torn coriander**
- **2 teaspoons sugar**
- **juice of 2 limes**
- **salt and pepper**

Skin the avocados and remove the pips. Mash the flesh with a fork. Mix in the remaining ingredients. Adjust the seasoning and add more lime juice if necessary. Set aside.

TIP: Limes are ideal for the Mexican flavours, but they can be tricky to find. Lemons will work just fine.

THE BLACKENED PEPPERS

- **several assorted peppers**

Grill your peppers directly over the flames, turning every now and then. Cook until the skin blackens.

Remove and place in a plastic bag, closing the bag so that the peppers sweat. When cooled, peel the skins away, rip into pieces and discard the seeds.

Place the peppers in a bowl and serve as a side dish with the tortillas.

TIP: When removing the skins from the peppers, don't rinse them under a tap. It will wash a lot of the flavour away.

THE TORTILLAS

- **12 flour tortillas**
- **1 tub crème fraîche**
- **grated cheddar**

To assemble, place a scoop of tomato salsa onto each tortilla. Top with the grilled and sliced tuna loin and finish with a dollop of crème fraîche, guacamole and grated cheddar cheese. Garnish with some extra coriander. Roll and eat.

Serve with extra tomato salsa and blackened peppers on the side.

My seafood prayers are answered, and what follows is a meal fresh from the ocean.

REUBEN RIFFEL

Ricotta gnocchi with gorgonzola sauce
Slow-baked lamb shanks
Sticky root vegetables & Tomato salad
Roast pears with brandy and almond cream

Reuben Riffel is probably the closest thing we've got to a celebrity chef in this country. But it's hard not to love the guy. He just seems to dig cooking.

Not only running the self-named, and highly acclaimed, Reuben's in Franschhoek, he also opened a spin-off at The Robertson Small Hotel. His latest project is his most ambitious yet and sees him stepping into the One and Only Hotel to replace Maze. It's a huge deal. Unlike Gordon Ramsay (who owns the Maze brand), Reuben understands that a big name isn't enough to make a place successful. As a result he splits his time between his venues, and is on site as much as possible. He is a busy, busy dude.

Franschhoek is still home though, and Reuben is in love with the town. It's in his blood. With his great-grandparents having arrived there in the late 1800s, his family has lived there ever since. Indeed, many of Reuben's childhood memories have formed the backbone of his unique style of cooking, which sees comfort food elevated to gourmet levels. Flavours are steeped in tradition, and his Malay-inspired dishes inject some much-needed "South African-ness" into his new venue.

We're a bit unsure about whether or not we've got the right address as we pull up to the house. We're greeted by two beautiful Shar-Pei dogs and I manage to catch the one's name on the tag. It reads "Szechuan". Something tells me this is the place. Reuben's wife, Maryke, welcomes us and shows us into the kitchen. Herself a qualified chef, she's busy preparing a starter and says we should make ourselves at home. The house is a beauty. Wide open doors lead us onto an outdoor deck, revealing a beautifully-set table. It's the type of scene that seems to invite you in to settle down for a long afternoon.

We're admiring the autumn sun dripping onto a bright, waxy lemon tree in the backyard when Reuben appears with a few cold beers. "Let's kick off," he says. And that's that. The doorbell rings and guests stream in. Reuben pours wine, chops vegetables and carries plates.

One thing is obvious: hospitality is a habit in this house, not a burden.

As I chat to Maryke in the kitchen, she reveals semolina as the secret to her gnocchi. I get to taste it straight from the pot and it's hard to leave some for the others. Semolina might be an ingredient, but love, patience and talent might be factors too.

The rest of the food is as good. Lamb shanks are baked instead of braised, resulting in sticky fingers from pulling the meat apart, while root vegetables are kept rustic. It's simple food that everyone dives into, and for a few seconds conversation comes to a standstill when it's put down at the table. Nobody talks. Everybody just eats.

We get the last few shots and say our goodbyes. Just as I suspected, everyone else seems to be settling in at that damn table. Can you hear I'm a bit jealous? Can you? Because I am.

RICOTTA GNOCCHI

WITH GORGONZOLA SAUCE | SERVES 4 – 6

THE GNOCCHI
- **400 g ricotta**
- **3 organic egg yolks**
- **2 tablespoons freshly grated Parmesan**
- **5 tablespoons semolina**
- **¼ teaspoon salt**
- **¼ teaspoon black pepper**
- **freshly grated nutmeg**
- **1 tablespoon finely chopped fresh flat leaf parsley**

Mix the ricotta, egg yolks, Parmesan (the pre-grated stuff will not do), semolina, salt, pepper and a couple of good pinches of nutmeg in a large bowl, and mix thoroughly to make dough.

On a lightly oiled surface (you could use a plastic tray or large chopping board if you don't want to oil your work surface), roll the dough into thin sausages about as thick as your thumb. Cut the rolls with a sharp knife into lengths about 2 cm long. Set aside while you prepare the sauce.

When the sauce is just about ready, bring a large pan of salted water to the boil and adjust the heat so that the water simmers gently (do not let it boil). Lower the gnocchi, one batch at a time, on a slotted spoon into the simmering water and poach until they float back to the surface – about 2 minutes.

Remove with a slotted spoon to a warmed serving dish. Drop more dumplings into the pan. Repeat the process until all your dumplings are cooked.

To serve, spoon the gnocchi onto plates or bowls. Briefly warm through the sauce and pour over the gnocchi. To garnish, sprinkle with the finely chopped parsley.

TIP: These gnocchi can be made a day ahead. They must be kept covered and in single layers, not touching, in the refrigerator, and cooked just before serving.

THE SAUCE
- **1 tablespoon butter**
- **2 tablespoons double cream**
- **100 g gorgonzola cheese, crumbled**

Melt the butter with the cream in a saucepan over low heat. Add the gorgonzola and squash and stir with a wooden spoon until you have a thick and creamy mixture (about 1 minute). Turn off the heat but keep warm until you are ready to serve the gnocchi.

SLOW-BAKED LAMB SHANKS

SERVES 4

- 8 sprigs rosemary
- 2 sprigs fresh thyme
- 150g cold butter
- 20g sage leaves
- sea salt and freshly cracked black pepper
- 4 lamb shanks, crown- or French-trimmed (ask your butcher to do this)
- 12 cloves garlic, peeled and finely sliced
- 1 onion, peeled and finely sliced
- olive oil
- dry white wine

Preheat your oven to 180 °C. Pick the leaves off half of the rosemary and thyme and whizz them in a food processor, along with the butter and most of the sage. Season well with salt and pepper. (If you don't have a food processor, just chop the herbs very finely and combine with the butter.)

Using a small knife, take one of the shanks and cut between the meat and the bone from the base of the shank upwards. You want to create a hole big enough to put your finger in, forming a pocket. Repeat for all the shanks.

Divide the butter between the shanks, pushing it into the created pockets. (This technique will give an incredible, rich flavour directly to the heart of the meat.)

Tear off four arm-length pieces of tinfoil and fold each in half to leave you with four A3-sized pieces of foil. Divide the sliced garlic and onion between them, making a pile in the middle of each square. Rub the lamb shanks with olive oil, season with salt and pepper and place on top of the onion pile. Add a sprig of rosemary and some sage leaves to each shank.

Carefully pull up the sides of the foil and add a splash of wine to each parcel. Gather the foil around the bone, pinching it together tightly. Excess foil can be trimmed with scissors. Repeat for all the shanks.

Place them on a baking tray, bones facing up. Cook for 2½ hours.

Unwrap and serve with roasted root vegetables and a tomato salad. (See recipes on page 195.)

STICKY ROOT VEGETABLES

SERVES 4

- ¼ cup olive oil
- a knob of butter
- 1 – 2 turnips, cut into
  3 cm pieces
- 5 – 6 parsnips, halved
  lengthways
- 500 g small, waxy potatoes
- 1 large bunch of baby carrots,
  each trimmed
- 6 – 8 baby onions, each
  trimmed
- salt and pepper
- 20 g roughly chopped flat
  leaf parsley
- mustard

Preheat your oven to 190 °C. Spoon olive oil and butter into a large roasting pan and heat in the oven until the butter is melted (about 1 minute). Add the vegetables, season to taste and stir to make sure everything is well combined.

Roast until the vegetables are tender and beginning to brown and crisp. (You can test with a skewer.) Scatter the parsley over the vegetables and top with your favourite mustard. Give them a stir to make sure everything gets a good coating of sauce, and serve.

A perfect accompaniment for lamb shanks (page 193).

TOMATO SALAD

SERVES 4 – 6

- 2 red onions, finely sliced
- 6 – 8 rosa tomatoes, halved
- 20 g flat leaf parsley, leaves only
- 20 g chervil, leaves only
- 3 tablespoons extra virgin
  olive oil (the best you can get
  your hands on)
- 1 tablespoon red wine vinegar
- salt and black pepper
- ½ cup good-quality, freshly
  grated Parmesan

Place the red onion, the tomatoes and the herbs in a bowl. Whisk the olive oil and the vinegar in a separate bowl until combined.

Pour the dressing over the salad, season with salt and black pepper, and finish off with a mountain of Parmesan. Serve as a side dish.

ROAST PEARS

WITH BRANDY AND ALMOND CREAM | SERVES 6

THE ALMOND CREAM
- 150 g blanched almonds
- 60 g castor sugar
- 300 ml cream
- 125 ml milk
- 6 egg yolks
- 40 ml amaretto

NOTE: The brandy and almond cream is more like a custard, but so rich and smooth, I had to call it a "cream". This recipe will make about 400 ml.

THE PEARS
- 10 fresh bay leaves
- 6 small, firm pears
- 6 small lemons
- 150 g castor sugar
- 100 g unsalted butter, coarsely chopped
- 75 ml extra virgin olive oil
- 150 ml brandy

NOTE: New-season pears are perfect for this recipe. Texture is important here, so it's best to use slightly firm pears.

Prepare the almond cream first. Preheat the oven to 180 °C. Roast the blanched almonds on a baking tray until golden (4 to 5 minutes). Allow to cool and process with the sugar in a food processor until finely ground, then transfer to a heat-proof bowl.

Bring the cream and 80 ml milk to the boil in a saucepan. Pour over the almond mixture, stir to combine and leave to infuse for 40 minutes.

Lightly whisk the egg yolks, add the amaretto, then add the cream and almond mixture, and the remaining milk. Transfer to a saucepan and cook over medium-low heat, stirring continuously, until the mixture coats the back of a wooden spoon thickly (8 to 10 minutes).

Strain through a fine sieve into a bowl placed over ice and cool, then refrigerate until chilled (1 to 2 hours).

Prepare the pears – halve them and remove the cores, ideally with a melon baller. Preheat the oven to 140 °C. Place bay leaves in the base of a roasting tray large enough to fit the pears snugly, then top with the pears, cut-sides up.

Squeeze over a little lemon juice to stop the pears from going brown. Remove the peel of 3 lemons with a vegetable peeler and scatter around the pears. Sprinkle over the sugar, then dot over butter, making sure some butter is in the core of each pear. Squeeze over more lemon juice, drizzle with olive oil and roast for 40 minutes.

Remove from the oven and baste the pears with the pan juices. Drizzle over the brandy, return to the oven and roast until tender (40 minutes). Increase the oven temperature to 160 °C. Remove and baste the pears, then return to the oven again and roast until caramelised (15 to 20 minutes).

Serve immediately with the almond cream and drizzle with the pan juices.

RICHARD CARSTENS

Smoked tofu and walnut pâté
Cabbage rolls and tempura mushrooms with dashi ponzu sauce
Miso cob with ginger salsa
Japanese salad | Bonito-flaked aubergine | Sesame potato salad
Green tea and lime tart

I'm sweating as I arrive at Richard Carstens's home. Not because it's hot. Rather because I know that it'll be my job to try to explain how beautiful this place is. I knew then what I know now: I will struggle to do it justice.

We've just driven past Tokara, where Richard spearheads one of the most exciting kitchens in the country, and have turned off the beaten track to arrive at the cottage he shares with his wife Tracy. Their "backyard" is a farm and, instead of a flower garden, a field of wild, pink proteas juts out of long grass. Soft light loops through the flowers and casts a dappled effect on the porch, like some kind of shadowed tablecloth that has been taken to with a shotgun. It's pretty special.

It's no secret that Richard is heavily influenced by Japanese culture, and some rad trinkets, collectibles and prints reflect this. The cottage breathes the same Zen-like coolness as its owners, and an iPod provides a perfectly chilled soundtrack for the afternoon. Music is a big deal for Richard, and the guy's got incredible taste. Well … if you can look past the Nick Cave obsession – his albums and books are scattered around the house. Indeed, music is a big part of the day's conversation and Richard talks about it with the same passion that he does for food, art and literature.

With the proteas as a backdrop, it's ironic that Tracy herself is a florist. I discover quickly that she's a gifted cook too, as she brings out a "simple" snack of smoked tofu and walnut pâté. It's delicious, but very unusual. The type of thing that a veget … no … surely not. It couldn't be. Could it? My God. "Richard," I wade in "…Tracy's not a vegetarian is she?" He laughs. "Luckily not, no," is the measured response. "She's a pescatarian. But her love for food is as strong as any red-blooded meat-eater." Aaah, well played sir.

The lunch that follows proves Richard to be right. In fact, it's Tracy who seems to be head chef in this kitchen! Richard slots in as the perfect "sous", and soon some seriously interesting dishes are being brought out. Gorgeous fillets of cob are rubbed in miso, but it's the simple aubergine that steals the show. It's been sliced and dusted with bonito flakes, which react to the heat. They "dance" in the wind as it is placed on the table – I've never seen anything like it.

Along with that, light and delicate tempura mushrooms provide texture and even a simple potato salad is given the Asian treatment with a sprinkling of sesame seeds. Dessert draws on Richard's influences too, with a green tea and lime tart providing an awesome end to the meal.

Well … it's almost the end. Before we head back to the real world we take one last indulgent stroll around the property. The sun is setting now and, impossibly, those proteas look even more impressive. Like I said, it's tough to do them justice.

SMOKED TOFU AND WALNUT PÂTÉ

SERVES 4 – 6

- 1 leek, chopped
- 1 teaspoon finely chopped ginger
- 1 stalk celery, finely chopped
- 1 tablespoon olive oil
- 200 g smoked tofu, chopped
- 50 g walnuts
- 2 tablespoons chives, finely sliced

Sauté the leek, ginger and celery in olive oil until softened. Add the chopped tofu and walnuts, and cook gently until softened. Remove from the heat and allow to cool.

Blend to a smooth consistency and finish by stirring through extra olive oil and chopped chives. Serve with sliced radishes and Melba toast.

The spines of the books read:

HISTORY OF JAPAN
FLORAL ART OF JAPAN
CHILDREN'S DAYS IN JAPAN
JAPANESE NOH PLAYS
JAPANESE DRAMA
JAPANESE MUSIC
KIMONO
JAPANESE MUSIC
FAMILY LIFE IN JAPAN
FLORAL CALENDAR OF JAPAN
FAMILY LIFE IN JAPAN
JAPANESE EDUCATION
JAPANESE BUDDHISM
JAPANESE FOOD

CABBAGE ROLLS

AND TEMPURA MUSHROOMS WITH DASHI PONZU SAUCE | SERVES 4

THE PONZU SAUCE
- 1 teaspoon dashi stock powder dissolved in 200 ml warm water
- 8 tablespoons Kikkoman low sodium soya sauce
- 240 ml rice wine vinegar
- 8 tablespoons lemon juice

Combine all the ingredients and whisk to emulsify. Set aside and allow the flavours to develop.

THE STEAMED CABBAGE
- 2 heads Chinese cabbage
- olive oil, for shallow frying
- salt and black pepper
- 2 cloves garlic, finely sliced
- togarashi spice, to taste

Slice off the end of the cabbage and separate into leaves. Spread out a few pieces of tin foil, about 50 cm x 20 cm.

Arrange the leaves on the foil, a few on top of each other in each stack, so that they lie flat with an even thickness. Roll the cabbage leaf stacks tightly into cylinders, and roll the foil over them, pressing as you roll, so that the foil holds the cabbage rolls together. There should be no spaces between the leaves. Secure with string at 5 cm intervals, and cut the roll into slices between the string, leaving an exposed surface at either end.

Heat the olive oil and add the salt, pepper and garlic. Cook gently over medium heat. Stand the cabbage rolls upright in the pan and fry them gently until steamed. Sprinkle with togarashi spice and keep warm. Remove the foil just before serving.

THE TEMPURA BATTER
- 400 ml iced water
- 1 egg yolk
- 80 g plain flour
- 80 g rice flour
- 40 g cornflour

In a bowl, mix the iced water and the egg yolk. In a separate bowl, mix the flours.

Add the flours gradually to the egg mixture, aiming for a loose batter with lumps of unmixed flour. Keep in the fridge until you are ready to cook the mushrooms.

THE MUSHROOMS
- 320 g mixed, wild mushrooms (shiitake, shimeji, oyster), roughly chopped
- flour, for dusting
- oil, for frying

Wipe the mushrooms and dust in flour, shaking off any excess. Dip into the cold tempura batter and deep-fry in hot oil (180 °C) in batches until golden and crispy. Drain on kitchen paper.

Serve the mushrooms with dashi ponzu sauce and the steamed cabbage rolls.

MISO COB WITH GINGER SALSA

SERVES 4

THE MISO COB

- 80 ml sake, or dry sherry
- 80 ml mirin
- 250 g white miso
- 110 g castor sugar
- 4 fillets of cob (160 g each)
- olive oil

It's best to make the marinade a day ahead and allow your fish to take on all the flavour. Put the sake and mirin in a pan and boil to allow the alcohol to evaporate.

Turn to medium heat and add the miso slowly with a spoon, until completely incorporated.

Turn the heat to high and add the sugar in two batches. Stir the mixture until the sugar has dissolved. Remove from the heat and allow to cool.

Rub the marinade onto the cob fillets, cover and refrigerate overnight.

When you have prepared all your accompaniments, it's time to pan-roast the cob.

Remove the fish from the marinade and wipe most of the miso off. Pan-roast the cob fillets in olive oil, until crisp, and finish off in the oven at 150 °C until cooked.

Serve with the ginger salsa and various side dishes (such as Japanese salad, Bonito-flaked aubergine and Sesame potato salad – see pages 206 and 208 for recipes).

THE GINGER SALSA

- 100 g finely chopped red onion
- 25 g finely chopped ginger
- 5 tablespoons Kikkoman low sodium soya
- 8 tablespoons rice wine vinegar
- 4 tablespoons dashi stock
- 1 tablespoon chopped coriander
- 2 teaspoons sesame oil

Combine all the ingredients well and refrigerate overnight. This will allow the flavours to develop.

JAPANESE SALAD

THE DRESSING
- 100 ml olive oil
- 4 teaspoons mirin
- 4 teaspoons rice wine vinegar
- 2 teaspoons low-salt soya sauce
- ¼ teaspoon sugar

Mix the olive oil, mirin, vinegar, soya sauce and sugar together, and set aside.

THE SALAD
- ½ cucumber, shaved with a vegetable peeler
- 1 avocado, peeled, stoned and sliced
- 100 g mange tout, blanched
- 100 g edamame beans, blanched
- 1 green pear, sliced
- 100 g watercress
- 100 g rocket
- 2 nori sheets, toasted and cut into strips

Combine all the salad ingredients, except the nori, and toss in a bowl.

When you are ready to serve, dress the salad and top with the toasted nori.

Serve with Miso cob (see page 205 for recipe).

BONITO-FLAKED AUBERGINE

- 4 tablespoons soya sauce
- 8 tablespoons rice wine vinegar
- 4 teaspoons lime juice
- 4 medium aubergines, cut into quarters and brushed with olive oil
- 1 cup bonito flakes

Preheat your oven to 200 °C. Mix the soya sauce, rice vinegar and lime juice until well combined.

Place the aubergines on a baking tray and roast until browned and cooked. Drizzle with the soya mixture and keep warm until you are ready to serve.

Top with bonito flakes when serving. (By the way, if you have never encountered them, bonito flakes are air-dried fillets of smoked bonito fish, shaved into delicate flakes.)

Serve with Miso cob (see page 205 for recipe).

SESAME POTATO SALAD

SERVES 6 – 8 AS A SIDE DISH

THE DRESSING

– 1 teaspoon sesame paste
– 50 ml olive oil
– 1 teaspoon soya sauce
– 1 teaspoon sesame oil
– 25 g chopped Italian parsley

THE POTATOES

– 400 g baby potatoes, boiled
  and cooled
– 1 teaspoon toasted sesame seeds

Combine the dressing ingredients until emulsified. Pour over the cooked potatoes and toss gently to coat.

Sprinkle with sesame seeds and serve immediately. Serve with Miso cob (see page 205 for recipe).

GREEN TEA AND LIME TART

SERVES 8 – 10

THE SWEET PASTRY

- 200 g plain flour
- 120 g butter, chilled and coarsely chopped
- 60 g icing sugar
- 1 egg, beaten lightly (use only half the beaten egg)

Blitz the flour, butter and icing sugar in a food processor until fine crumbs form.

Add half the beaten egg and process further, until the mixture just comes together.

Turn the mixture out onto a floured work surface and bring it together with the heel of your hand. Form into a disc, wrap in plastic and refrigerate until firm.

When ready, roll out the pastry on a floured surface until about 2 mm thick. Use it carefully to line a lightly greased 26 cm diameter tart case. Trim all edges and refrigerate until firm.

Preheat the oven to 180 °C and blind bake the tart case, using baking beans or weights to prevent the pastry from puffing up while it cooks.

When golden brown, remove from the oven and allow to cool.

THE FILLING

- 375 ml cream
- finely grated zest and juice of 3 limes
- 1 vanilla bean, split and seeds scraped out
- 1 tablespoon green tea powder
- 13 egg yolks
- 185 g castor sugar
- 110 ml sake
- 1 teaspoon cornflour

Preheat your oven to 150 °C. Combine the cream, lime zest, vanilla bean and seeds, and the green tea powder in a saucepan. Bring to the boil.

Remove from the heat and let stand for 30 minutes to allow the flavours to infuse.

Whisk the egg yolks, sugar, sake and lime juice in a heat-proof bowl until well combined. Bring the cream mixture back to the boil and pour over the egg yolk mixture.

Whisking quickly, add the cornflour. Return the mixture to the pan and stir continuously over low heat until it thickly coats the back of a wooden spoon.

Strain the mixture into the pastry case and bake until set (10 to 12 minutes).

Serve the tart with a simple ice cream – something like almond works well.

VANESSA MARX

The ultimate Pimm's sundowner / Yellowtail ceviche
Seared free-range beef fillet with porcini mushrooms and gremolata
Madeleines with roasted nectarines, honey and clotted cream

At the time of writing I guess it's safe to file Vanessa Marx in the "rising stars" category. A year later (by the time you're reading this) she'll be sitting amongst the best chefs in the country. Trust me. As the youngest chef in this book (26 years old), Vanessa's also one of the most interesting. Having been diagnosed with diabetes at the age of fifteen, she was forced to make some major adjustments regarding her relationship with food. However, instead of seeing her condition as something holding her back from cooking and eating freely, she chose to explore food in more detail. The result is a seriously talented chef.

As the head chef at Dear Me – one of the more exciting restaurants to pop up in Cape Town in recent times – Vanessa is out to prove that healthy food doesn't need to taste like … well … healthy food. To do this, she's developed a style that is easy to spot. Flavours are light, clean and balanced. Dishes have only a handful of ingredients. Cooking time is limited where possible, with natural textures being maintained. Every dish is plated beautifully and showcases the produce that Vanessa goes out of her way to source. The meat is free-range, the fish is sustainable, fruit and vegetables are seasonal.

This is a chef who was forced to acknowledge how important whatever goes into her body is, and through a daily-changing menu she's showing her customers how to become a bit more aware too.

Vanessa's invited us to come and hang out at her birthday party. Her boyfriend Blake's parents have a house in Noordhoek and she explains that she spends "every single weekend" out there. When we arrive, Vanessa is busy with some finishing touches before the rest of the guests arrive. She's a machine. In between lighting lanterns and pouring cocktails, she fires up the braai, grabs a pair of tongs and throws on two huge fillets. This chick is not afraid to get her hands dirty. The multi-tasking exhibition continues as she proceeds to plate up a fresh yellowtail ceviche, dressed with chilli and avocado. In fact, she does this so quickly that we've finished shooting it before the meat has even cooked. This is Vanessa at her best. No unnecessary ingredients or complications; just brilliant produce and well thought-out flavours.

That meat is done pretty soon. "We don't eat meat well done in this house," laughs Vanessa, as she slaps it down on a board and carries it to the kitchen. In less than 10 minutes she's back out. The meat has been sliced and tossed with glorious porcini mushrooms, simply pan-fried in a knob of butter. A handful of rocket and some pine nuts are thrown into the mix, while the whole thing is finished off with Parmesan shavings and a trickle of truffle oil.

The light is fading and, as I try to calm a nervous photographer, Vanessa produces her dessert. Handmade madeleines with roasted nectarines and some impossibly thick clotted cream. It's another show-stopper. Vanessa has miraculously pulled off three dishes (and some cocktails) with plenty of time to spare. Diabetes shmiabetes.

213

THE ULTIMATE PIMM'S SUNDOWNER

SERVES 2

- 2 slices orange
- 2 slices lime
- 4 strawberries
- 4 raspberries
- 6 cherries
- 2 cucumber sticks
- 2 sprigs fresh mint
- ice
- 6 tots Pimm's
- 250 ml soda water
- 250 ml lemonade
- 200 ml verjuice

Take 2 jam jars (500 ml) and put a slice of orange, a slice of lime, a strawberry, 2 raspberries, 3 cherries, a cucumber stick and a sprig of mint into each. Add a large handful of ice and 3 tots of Pimm's to each jar.

Fill each jar with 125 ml soda, 125 ml lemonade and 100 ml verjuice. Make a slit in each of the extra strawberries and wedge them onto the top of the jars to garnish. Mix with a straw and serve immediately.

CHEF'S NOTE: I like to use sugar-free lemonade. Fruit-wise just go with whatever you fancy really.

YELLOWTAIL CEVICHE

WITH FRESH PEAS, AVOCADO, CHILLI AND LIME | SERVES 4

- 800 g fresh yellowtail fillet, skinned, deboned and cut away from the bloodline
- 100 g fresh peas
- 1 red chilli
- 80 ml extra virgin olive oil
- 1 large avocado
- 20 g fresh coriander, washed
- juice of 4 limes
- mixed salad leaves, to serve
- salt and black pepper, to taste
- 4 additional limes, quartered (for serving)

Using a sharp filleting knife, slice the 2 yellowtail fillets into 1 mm slices. Try to slice at an angle. This will give you a bigger surface area for each slice. Arrange the slices of fish on a large plate or platter.

Blanch your peas in boiling, salted water for 20 seconds only (no more). Remove with a slotted spoon and plunge into a pre-prepared bowl filled with iced water. This will prevent them from cooking further, and will help them retain their colour. Leave them in the ice water for 2 minutes until chilled, and then strain off the ice water.

Chop the chilli very finely and mix into the olive oil. Cut the avocado in half and remove the pip and skin, before cutting each half into cubes.

Arrange the avocado, coriander leaves and blanched peas over the slices of ceviche, before dressing generously with the chilli oil and lime juice.

Add a handful of mixed greens and season with salt and pepper. Serve with the lime quarters.

CHEF'S NOTE: I pride myself on using only SASSI green-listed fish, and find yellowtail a perfect candidate for this dish. If it's not available try angelfish, which also works well.

SEARED FREE-RANGE BEEF FILLET

WITH PORCINI MUSHROOMS AND GREMOLATA | SERVES 8

THE GREMOLATA
- 1 lemon
- 30 g Italian flat leaf parsley, washed
- 2 cloves garlic, finely chopped

To make the gremolata, zest the lemon with a microplane citrus zester or use the fine side of a grater. Set aside the lemon to be used later.

Meanwhile, finely chop the parsley and mix together with the lemon zest and the chopped garlic.

THE BEEF
- 1 large, whole free-range beef fillet (about 1.5 kg)
- salt and pepper, to taste
- extra virgin olive oil, to taste

The best way to cook this beef is, surprisingly, on a gas barbeque. Turn the gas on the highest setting and close the lid to let it heat up. Season the beef fillet generously with salt and freshly ground black pepper, and give it a rub with a splash of olive oil. Once the barbeque is heated up to around 220 °C, put the whole fillet on the grill and close the lid.

Let it cook on the first side for 2 minutes, then turn the fillet a third of the way around, close the lid and cook for a further 2 minutes. Repeat the process one more time. After a total cooking time of 6 minutes, take the fillet off the grill and leave it to rest on a chopping board.

THE MUSHROOMS
- 500 g fresh porcini mushrooms
- a little oil
- 50 g unsalted butter
- salt and pepper, to taste

Slice the porcini mushrooms lengthways. Heat a large frying pan and drizzle with a little oil. Add in the porcini, season with salt and pepper, and fry until golden brown. Turn off the heat and add the butter, letting it melt over the mushrooms.

TO SERVE
- 100 g wild rocket, washed
- 200 g local, mature Parmesan
- 100 g pine nuts, toasted
- 2 tablespoons white truffle oil

Slice the fillet into pieces about 1 cm thick and arrange them on a large platter. Toss the fried porcini on top, and scatter over the rocket leaves. Using a vegetable peeler, shave the Parmesan over the beef and porcini. Sprinkle with the pine nuts and gremolata, before drizzling the truffle oil over the entire dish.

Give it a final seasoning with salt and freshly ground black pepper, as well as a generous drizzle of olive oil and a squeeze of lemon juice (from the lemon kept aside from the gremolata). Serve immediately.

These little French sponges are
traditionally baked in a shell-shaped
mould. Madeleine moulds are available
from most good kitchen shops.

MADELEINES

WITH ROASTED NECTARINES, HONEY AND CLOTTED CREAM | SERVES 4

MADELEINES
- 75 g unsalted butter
- 100 g castor sugar
- zest of 1 orange
- 3 eggs
- 100 g cake flour
- 5 ml baking powder

Preheat the oven to 160 °C and spray the madeleine mould with a non-stick spray.

Using an electric mixer, cream together the butter and sugar, then add the orange zest. Beat the eggs into the mixture one by one, incorporating each one before adding the next.

Sift together the flour and baking powder, and carefully fold it into the butter mixture. Spoon a teaspoonful of batter into each little shell mould and bake for 10 minutes, or until a cake skewer comes out clean.

Remove the madeleines from the moulds and leave to cool on a cooling rack.

CLOTTED CREAM
- 250 ml fresh cream

TIP: You can simply buy clotted cream from a specialised deli, but this is a homemade version. Ideally it should be made the day before required.

Pour the cream into a saucepan, and put it onto a medium heat. Leave the cream on the heat until it has thickened and reduced by one third. When satisfied, pour the cream into a container and cover with a layer of cling film so that it touches the surface (to prevent a skin from forming).

Once cooled to room temperature, refrigerate overnight so that it has plenty of time to set.

THE NECTARINES
- 4 medium nectarines
- 50 g unsalted butter
- 50 g castor sugar
- 250 ml clotted cream
- toasted almond flakes (optional garnish)
- 4 tablespoons pure honey
- icing sugar, to serve

Preheat the oven grill to its highest setting. Cut the nectarines in half, and remove the pip. Place the nectarine halves in a roasting dish, with the cut side facing upwards.

Put a dot of butter into each nectarine and sprinkle with castor sugar, so that the nectarines are evenly covered. Roast them under the grill until slightly softened and golden brown.

Place 2 roasted nectarine halves and 2 madeleines into each dessert bowl. Spoon dollops of clotted cream over them and sprinkle with the toasted almonds.

Drizzle with honey and give a generous dusting of icing sugar before serving.

RECIPE INDEX

Page numbers in **bold** indicate that there is a photograph of the dish.

SUNBIRD PUBLISHERS

First published in 2012

Sunbird Publishers (Pty) Ltd
The illustrated imprint of Jonathan Ball Publishers
P O Box 6836
Roggebaai 8012
Cape Town, South Africa

www.sunbirdpublishers.co.za

Registration number: 1984/003543/07

Copyright published edition © Sunbird Publishers 2012
Copyright text 2012 © Andy Fenner
Copyright images 2012 © Lar Leslie

Design and typesetting by MR Design
Cover design by MR Design
Editing and project management by Michelle Marlin
Proofreading by Kathleen Sutton

Reproduction by Resolution Colour, Cape Town
Printed and bound by Tien Wah Press Pte Ltd (Singapore)

ISBN 978-1-920289-56-0

While every last effort has been made to check that information in this recipe book is correct at the time of going to press, the publisher, author and their agents will not be held liable for any damages incurred through any inaccuracies.